ROGER COLE

Burning to speak

Overleaf: Head of a Young Man, 1912 (enlarged, see p. 56)

ROGER COLE

Burning to speak

THE LIFE AND ART OF **HENRI GAUDIER BRZESKA**

Phaidon
OXFORD

Phaidon Press Limited, Littlegate House, St Ebbe's Street, Oxford

Published in the United States of America
by E. P. Dutton, New York

First published 1978
© 1978 Phaidon Press Limited
All rights reserved

ISBN 0 7148 1850 4
Library of Congress Catalog Card Number 78–55006

Printed in Great Britain by Jolly & Barber Limited, Rugby

CONTENTS

To Elizabeth, Rachel and Christopher

Foreword

Reference has been made to the three different authors who have published books concerning the life and work of Henri Gaudier. Since some of these books have been reissued in various editions, it is essential to establish which texts have been used and to explain their abbreviation. The following references have been used:

Ede, 1:	*Savage Messiah* by H. S. Ede, Heinemann, 1931
Ede, 2:	*A Life of Gaudier Brzeska* by H. S. Ede, Heinemann, 1930
Brodzky, 1:	*Henri Gaudier Brzeska* by H. Brodzky, Faber & Faber, 1933
Brodzky, 2:	*Gaudier Brzeska.* Drawings by H. Brodzky. Faber & Faber, 1946
Pound, 1:	*Gaudier Brzeska* by E. Pound, Allen Lane 1916
Pound, 2:	*Gaudier Brzeska* by E. Pound. Reprint. Marvel Press 1960

Acknowledgements

The author and publishers would like to thank all those museums and private individuals who have given permission for works in their possession to be reproduced, and special thanks to Horst Kolo who was responsible for much of the photography. The following have kindly lent photographic material: London, Tate Gallery, 2, 5, 21a & b, 25, 28, 30a, 43, 55, 57, 60, 63b, 67; London, National Portrait Gallery, p. 25; London, Victoria and Albert Museum, 7, 29, 36; London, Fine Art Society Limited, 24; Cambridge, Kettle's Yard, 2, 011, 012, 036; Liverpool, Walker Art Gallery, 22; Doncaster, Museum and Art Gallery, 10; Bristol, City Art Gallery, 37; University of Hull, 11; Leeds Art Gallery, 12; Cardiff, National Museum of Wales, 7, 20; Manchester, City Art Gallery, 27; Chicago, Art Institute, Gift of Samuel Lustgarten, 26, 52; New York, Museum of Modern Art, 68; Yale, University Art Gallery, 51; Boston, Museum of Fine Arts, Otis Norcross Fund, 42; Minneapolis, Minn., Walker Art Center, 35; Orléans, Musée des Beaux-Arts, 1; Ottowa, National Gallery of Canada, 21; David C. Golby, 38; Anthony d'Offay, 16; Gillian Raffles, The Mercury Gallery, 54, 63a, Judith Wolfe, 46, 53.

1

THE FORMATIVE YEARS

1891 *to* 1911

Henri Gaudier was born on 4 October 1891 at St-Jean de Braye, near Orléans, France. By trade his father was a carpenter and joiner, and, although he claimed to be 'ni intellectual ni un grammarien',[1] the influences he had on the early development of his son were all-important. His own description of his attitudes towards his son best explain the significance of this:

Nous avons élève notre fils dans l'amour de la liberté et nous aimions a discûter avec lui même sur des choses insignificatives et nous l'encouragions à défendre avec perseverance ce qui lui semblait juste, jusqu'à preuve irrefutable du contraire, nos petites-discûtions prenaient d'avantage d'importance à mésure qu'il s'élevait en age et en raison.[2]

Through this attitude, his love of the countryside, animals and insects, and his employment as a craftsman, Gaudier's father moulded a particular environment for his son. The young Gaudier, however, was not a strong boy: frail and anaemic in appearance, though alert and inquisitive in manner. His father recalled his particular fascination for examining and drawing insects, drawings which he would destroy as soon as he had done them. When questioned about this he would reply: 'Je les ait[sic] fait celà me suffit, si je les gardais, je serais tente de les refaire et celà me serais, plûtot nuisible.'[3]

In 1897 he started school in St-Jean de Braye under the instruction of a M. Pointoise, and from the start his academic ability seemed above average. His progress at school was rapid; he readily assimilated ideas above his age ability and this was considered the more extraordinary because of his working-class background.[4] In October 1903 he moved to the Benjamin Franklin School in Orléans where he continued to make rapid progress. Particular abilities began to develop, one of which was in

languages, and, as a direct result of the interest shown by his teacher M. Roux, Gaudier gained his first academic award, which was a trip to London in June and July of 1906 to study English. This was his first visit abroad and undoubtedly gave him opportunities which he put to good use on his return, since within twelve months he had won a second scholarship worth three thousand francs to study business methods abroad for two years.

Throughout these years of secondary education his creative talents had not been idle, but nor had they been encouraged; his parents had great hopes that he would make a success of a business career. It seems likely, however, that he painted in his spare time, enjoyed rambles through the countryside with his father and learnt how to handle the carpenter's tools his father used at work.

In September 1907, Gaudier came to England for his second visit, living in Bristol with Mr George Smith, a friend of M. Roux, who taught at the Merchant Venturers College, where Gaudier was to study. It was with some surprise that the family discovered that not only was he academically capable but also artistic. Kitty Smith, a daughter of Mr Smith, particularly remembered this:

While he was with us he was always fond of painting and although he had nothing but a child's box of paints — about six paints in one row and six paints in another row — even with my family's small knowledge of painting, one could see that his work was quite outstanding. My father was astounded when he saw it first. He didn't do anything except watercolours and pencil drawings. We used to go for bicycle rides in the country quite a lot, and he always had a sketchbook in his pocket, and anything that interested him, he produced the sketchbook and sketched it. But he didn't keep any of them — everything was torn

Henri Gaudier aged 15

up. . . . He was interested in country life, he knew all the animals around St-Jean de Braye. He was very interested in moths and butterflies and had some rare specimens. I think that came through his father . . . when my brother and I were staying in Orléans in 1913 we went for a day to see the Gaudiers and the father took us for a long walk round the country and he told us the name of all the flowers, the trees, the animals, the birds, everything he saw, so that I feel is where Gaudier got his love of the country life.[5]

Gaudier seems to have enjoyed both the company of Kitty and his year at the school. The sketchbooks which survive from this period are the first record of his creative ability and talent at this age. The drawings show a meticulous study of local architecture, and the subjects, which are drawn in pen and ink, are sketched with a tightly controlled line. All these drawings are carefully signed and dated and it is evident from the choice of subject, which also included animals, birds and flowers, that he was unconcerned about style and preoccupied with achieving true representation.

With the completion of the academic year, Gaudier took his sketchbook on holiday to Devon and Somerset and on another short visit to London; it is in these drawings, and in the architectural, animal and plant studies he completed on his return to Bristol in August, that we can see the first indications of a developing fluency of line. He spent the latter part of September drawing in Bristol Museum and here again there is evidence of a more confident and critical approach to drawing.

In late September he left Mr and Mrs Smith for Cardiff to complete the second part of his scholarship in commerce: his employer was Mr Ching, of Fifoot and Ching, a coal exporting company. The most important record of his life in Cardiff has been written by Mr Ching himself:

He was one of several students who came to us, and whilst he excellently fulfilled the duties allotted to him, one could easily notice that his mind was not altogether on his work. Art undoubtedly occupied the greater part of it, and in his spare moments he was everlastingly, pencil or pen in hand, sketching some little incident that appealed to him. During his lunch hours he periodically walked across to the docks, and brought back with him a small sketch of, perhaps, the bow of a boat, or the elevation of a crane or tip, all of which showed genius. I encouraged him in this work because I felt that commerce was not his forte, and that he should be bound to leave it at the first possible chance. . . . In character he was somewhat Bohemian, and just a little casual, which was natural, but he was the kind of boy that one would have expected, if necessary, to have lived in a garret while he got on with his life's work as he felt it to be.[6]

Alfred Hazell, who was also employed by Mr Ching, recalled:

Gaudier was the third of a succession of French youths, winners of scholarships offered by the French Government, sent over to study English, and employed (at little or no salary) by the small coal exporting firm for which I worked. I have never lost the impression of the mysterious power he left with me and have wondered a thousand times in the years that have passed since I saw him, in what particular way he had distinguished himself, knowing well that he could hardly fail to make his mark in the world. Henri Alphonse Seraphim Mari Gaudier, he called himself, and all that time spent virtually all of his time drawing, with a special passion for pen and ink pictures of bits of old churches, and Ruskin was his guide.[7]

The reference to Ruskin confirms that he had by this time become concerned with his style of drawing. He sketched in the docks, in the parks and in Cardiff Museum. The sketches of this 1908/9 period are more adventurous than the controlled architectural studies done earlier in Bristol, and have in addition a vitality which is chiefly the result of a variation in his use of cross-hatching and line. The drawings display a conscious search in developing a concise means of expression using charcoal and pen, and this is well exemplified in the large number of drawings of birds and animals.[8] Surprisingly, the architectural studies of this period, Caerphilly Castle and Llandaff Cathedral,[9] show little development from the Bristol studies of architecture, but with the animals in the parks and in the docks he found a new freedom in the very nature of the subject, resulting in his most expressive drawings to date.

In April 1909, his 'employment' with Fifoot and Ching was completed, but before he left England, he visited Mr and Mrs Smith again (12 April), then travelled to London, sketching even on the train, and spent the day of the 16th drawing at the British Museum.[10] On 17 April he left London via Paris, Antwerp and Cologne for Nürnberg, recording his journey in a sketchbook. On 20 April he arrived at the house of Dr Uhlemayr, a friend of M. Roux who had been involved in organizing Gaudier's travelling scholarship.

Dr Uhlemayr's home provided another academic background within which Gaudier could learn. Mr Smith had stimulated and provoked intelligent and philosophical thinking in Cardiff. Dr Uhlemayr now acted as tutor, patron and confidant in Nurnberg.

Gaudier's stay in Germany is equal to, if not more important than the year he spent in Bristol. His fluency with the German language improved and he spent most of his time studying and reading, and sketched everything that interested him. In March 1929 Dr Uhlemayr remembered his visit with obvious sentiment:

It was amazing how quickly he learnt German. He could understand everything after a fortnight, and was fairly good at talking, so that one could converse with him about everything in German. We were surprised at his talent for languages, and his extraordinary gifts and mental richness were also evident. I discussed art and cultural questions with him and found in him an astonishing

Drawing of a heron, Cardiff, 1908

Drawing of Cardiff Docks, 1908

understanding for all problems of this sort. He obviously felt that he was helped by his conversations with me. . . . He took up my opinions greedily, without however making himself a slave to them, but on the contrary worked them around in his way and used them as elements in his own view of life. For as long as he was here, he wanted to be a painter, and he practised indefatigably at it.[11] More often he said when alone that he doubted that he was destined to be a painter and thought that drawing would be his only art; at the same time he said that actually he was a sculptor. So the genius in him struggled for clarity.

During this time he visited Munich, a trip which helped him considerably. He studied the city's art treasures, and particularly concerned himself with Munich arts and crafts, which he greatly treasured. His judgements on art and culture, of which you will find much in his letters and sketchbooks, are astonishingly rich and full for one of his age.[12]

Gaudier was in Munich by July at the latest, and in his continued correspondence with Kitty enthused about the galleries, libraries and the royal collection of engravings, and in one letter concluded: 'I am now so far in Art as to be able to go in for illustration as soon as I am in Paris.'[13] It is not certain when he left Munich, but with the help of a M. Simonet he had started work in Paris by the end of October, typing and translating letters with A. Colin, a publisher. The work did not satisfy him at all and when he wrote to Dr Uhlemayr again he explained his dilemma. 'Ten hours of each day I have to do translations and letters in a bookshop, which you will agree is a pretty poor lookout: the rest of the time I work for my own pleasure — I am trying to perfect my drawing and hope to succeed. . . . I've made immense strides since I was with you but how small they seem beside those I must still make. Every evening I work in the St Géneviève Library.'[14]

By the end of 1909, at the age of eighteen, Gaudier seemed poised to make a successful ascent of the commercial ladder, his undoubted ability in languages giving him a real advantage over many of his contemporaries. But his heart was not in commerce, and he had the problem of how to extricate himself from a career chosen for him by his parents. How could he continue to placate his parents and take up art as a full-time occupation? The fact that he should even have thought in these terms is astonishing: as yet he still had no formal training in art and was only self-taught.

He needed some reassurance, someone whose support would enable him to make a break with family ideals and take up art. Consequently, on 1 January, Gaudier wrote to Dr Uhlemayr; and here, for the first time, he wrote about sculpture. Unfortunately, we have knowledge only of those parts of the letters that have already been published, but it reveals that his knowledge and understanding of sculpture was still very limited, limited in fact to the Classical and to Rodin:

'We will never see a greater sculptor than Rodin, who has exhausted himself trying to surpass Phidias; he succeeded in his *Thinker*, but this success he will never surpass. Rodin is for France what Michelangelo was for Florence, he will have imitators but never rivals. . . . It is fatal; for these men by their monstrous personality bleed a nation to death and leave others only the alternatives of imitation or veneration.'[15]

It was while studying at the St Génevieve Library in Paris that Gaudier met a Polish woman called Sophie Brzeska, twenty years older than he, and during the early months of 1910 an understanding developed between them. Although absorbed in his studies in the Paris libraries and in the Louvre, Gaudier was lonely, as were many other students, and the interest shown in his studies by Miss Brzeska gave him encouragement. Sophie Brzeska professed to understand his loneliness and as they began to meet more frequently she gave him the encouragement he searched for — encouragement to study art.

Ezra Pound states that it was as a result of conversations at this time with a Czech poet, whom he had met at the Café Cujas, that Gaudier became determined to devote himself to sculpture.[16] From the many references in diaries and notebooks by both Sophie and Gaudier we know that they spent many hours at this café and in the rue Cujas, where Sophie had lodgings. They excitedly discussed their ideas on art and philosophy with each other and with many of the foreign students they met. The sketchbook, *Le Chaos*, quoted by Pound[17] is probably of this date and it seems likely that in addition to his new interests in sculpture Gaudier also started to read books which particularly interested Sophie. Certainly this new friendship gave a great lift to his ego and to his enthusiasm and interest in learning. Sophie was well-read, and together they explored aspects of art and literature. Sophie did not resolve all the problems however; money was short, yet he tried desperately to find a way to give up his job but still earn enough money to continue to study art. On 5 March he again wrote to Dr Uhlemayr of his troubles:

During this last week I have been the 'theater' of a great battle. On one side happiness and nature represented by the simple life of the fields and on the other the sadness and artificiality of commerce and town life. The pleasure of the fields is clouded by bad weather, by danger to the harvest, but, in spite of this, happiness remains, no less truly. The misery of commerce, though tempered by art, is the enemy of pleasure. The two things: nature, a superhuman and beautiful creation, and the town, human and ugly, these will always keep their peculiar characteristics.

The exigencies of life compel man to obtain money. Commerce provides this but I cannot face it and since art doesn't bring any money I am inclined to abandon this life of a middleman robber which repels me and will do all that I can to learn some craft which will dissipate the idea that to produce nothing during the day is to waste my time. But I have decided nothing; the town and the fields sit opposite each other — and if I have a trade, I shall still need art. . . . One thing I can absolutely decide, it is the only thing I can cut off at once, namely to give up commerce for some craft work. I am going to learn the technique of sculpture in wood for cabinet-making. I shall give next month to do this and it is with this I hope to earn my daily bread and not by fleecing the masses. When I face the beauty of nature I am no longer sensitive to art, but in the town I appreciate its myriad benefits — the more I go into the woods and the fields the more distrustful I become of art and wish all civilization to the devil; the more I wander about amidst filth and sweat the better I understand art and love it; the desire for it becomes to me a crying need.[18]

Although this letter is romantically biased in favour of Dr Uhlemayr, it shows that Gaudier was beginning to struggle with a personal philosophy. This philosophy was determined through discussion with Sophie and at the same time influenced by many of the young, cosmopolitan students he met while working at the St Géneviève Library and relaxing in the Café Cujas. His thinking was still very idealistic, as is exemplified by the idea of 'cabinet-making'. His idea of working at this craft must have relied on the earlier knowledge gained from his father about woodworking, and in a letter to Kitty, later that year, Gaudier told her that he had carved a large picture frame, to earn some money, but there is nothing to suggest he did any other work to further this notion of earning a living from the craft.[19]

Soon afterwards Kitty Smith and her parents moved from Bristol to Rockingham near Uppingham, and, as a result of some prompting from her, Gaudier wrote apologizing for having let their correspondence lapse. From this letter we learn that he had left his job for the very reasons that he gave Dr Uhlemayr for not liking it: 'I am involved in trouble just now. The fierce rapaciousness and lust of lying tradesmen made me leave the publishing firm I was working for about twelve days ago — I am looking for other gallows but cannot find them. Let us hope that it will end for the better.'[20] Since he had hardly any money it was important he found another job quickly, and in his next letter to Kitty he told her that he had found work with a firm manufacturing 'gunsights and looking-glasses'.[21]

As well as keeping Kitty happy with chatty correspondence he was also under certain pressures from home. His parents obviously sensed the uneasiness which he felt in his work, but for his part he could not yet bring himself to tell them that he hated commerce and longed for the relative freedom of art. Consequently, rather than write letters which upset them, he found it easier to discuss his worries and ideas with Sophie and then rationalize and elaborate them in correspondence with Dr Uhlemayr and Kitty. Much of Gaudier's writing at this time examined a theme which had surfaced in his earliest letters and which recurred throughout his later life: hatred of the city and love of the countryside. He put this argument into many forms over the next few years, but he always seemed to be inextricably caught between wanting to be in one place and having to be in the other. But, at the end of May, a letter to Dr Uhlemayr contained his most important decision:

I have taken a great decision — I am not going to do any more colour work but will restrict myself entirely to the plastic. I have never been able to see colour detached from form, and this year, after doing a few studies in painting, I noticed that the drawing and the modelling were all I have been concerned with. I have put by the brushes and tubes and have snatched the chisel and the boaster — two simple instruments which most admirably second the most wonderful of modelling tools, the human thumbs. This and clay is all that I need now, with charcoal or red chalk and paper. Painting is too complicated with its oil and its pigments, and is too easily destroyed. What is more, I love the sense of creation, the ample voluptuousness of kneading the material and bringing forth life, a joy which I never found in painting for as you have seen I don't know how to manipulate colour.

You will have noticed that civilizations begin with sculpture and end with it; painting, music, letters are later refinements. . . . For my part I see quite clearly that I don't wish to wield the brush any longer, it's too monotonous and one cannot feel the material near enough; paint sticks well to the hairs of the brush and sings on the canvas, one appreciates its fertile texture, but the sensuous enjoyment is far greater when the clay slips through your hands, when you can feel how plastic it is, how thick, how well bound together, and when you see it constantly bringing forth.

I am now right in the midst of Bohemia, a queer and mystic group but happy enough, there are days when you have nothing to eat, but life is so full of the unexpected that I love it as much as before I used to detest the stupid and regular life of commercial employment.[22]

His thinking was sometimes confused, and in letters written at this time there are many conflicting ideas, but they reveal what kind of reading and thinking was taking place and give foundation to the seemingly impetuous and extravagant behaviour of later years. His anarchical ideas rapidly developed during his later months in Paris and it seems likely that since many of the avant-garde ideals and beliefs were new to him he enjoyed participation in all of them at the same time. He defined this period as transitional when he later wrote to Dr Uhlemayr, revealing how he was really involved in the philosophy rather than the practice of art.

I have been reading Taine's *Philosophy of Art*. His theory does not seem to me to be very sound; it is true that environment does have an influence, but what has a much greater effect on the artist is love or hatred. He uses his setting to express these things — that is how I see it. Take for example Forain — the best draughtsman in my opinion. This man has been made spiteful by the misery of his early years: he began his work in a spirit of implacable raillery against the customs and manners of his contemporaries; today the influence of his surroundings is modified enormously — he is rich. The setting has changed but the artist has become even more intransigent and malicious than before. His drawings breathe the strength of a perfect anarchy. This powerful personality dominating its surroundings is a thing which Taine never explains. I do not believe that it is possible or useful to describe art in so rigorously scientific a way. You know that I have given up painting. I have only a small talent for painting, better say none. I now only practise the plastic, of which the elementary form is drawing.

I have tried to place caricatures in the Parisian papers, they took a few for *Rire* and *Charivari* — I don't know if they published them but they paid well. I shall try again, particularly since my ideas have become more crisp and precise; but there is the difficulty — at nineteen one is scarcely more than a child and the battle is hard. One's line lacks snap and vigour and one's outlook is narrow — there is a want of cohesion. There are parts which seem free, original, and others which are full of outside influences and childishness. The editors see this clearly enough and it is better for their papers but it sometimes drives me to despair — still one has to sacrifice oneself a bit. One only has to take three vows — poverty, chastity, abstinence, and everything goes well, one leads the life of an ascetic and art alone inspires you — in addition you must develop by cultivating your personal energy par la culture de ses seules forces.[23]

This letter was idealistic and hopeful, but overwork, ill-health and undernourishment soon drove Gaudier from Paris to his parents' home at St-Jean de Braye. He did not stop working, and within a very short period of his arrival he had completed a number of portraits, including a self-portrait and bust of his father (No. 1).[24] But soon after this the family doctor forbade him to do any more sculpture whatsoever since he was on the verge of complete breakdown.

Sophie was also concerned for his welfare and moved down to St-Jean de Braye. Her arrival, and the fact that she lived in rented accommodation, was socially unsatisfactory to Gaudier's parents. She was eventually evicted from her rooms for entertaining Gaudier, and the

disgrace that this brought upon the family caused a domestic crisis from which Gaudier and his parents never fully recovered.[25] He left home with Sophie before Christmas, never to return.

The disastrous conclusion to 1910 left Gaudier with no real base to work from, and not surprisingly he returned to Sophie for support. On leaving his parents they had returned to Paris, but Gaudier felt betrayed not only by his parents but by France and as a result decided to go to England. This decision was possibly influenced by earlier happy memories, and he obviously placed great importance on the artistic opportunities which he anticipated in London. So, early in January 1911, they crossed over from France, knowing no one in London, and having very little money. Their optimism was rapidly shattered, Gaudier could not find employment, their lodgings were filthy and their only means of subsistence came from Sophie's savings.

It is not surprising that there are few or no drawings or sketches from these early months of 1911, since both of them were chiefly preoccupied with survival. Gaudier, however, was never really able to put his study of art on one side. It seems likely that his consuming interest in galleries and museums, and his continuous searches for interesting subjects to draw, were probably the only factors which kept him in London.

In March he at last acquired a job with a timber import-and-export company named after its owner, Wulfsberg. This employment provided him with £6 a month, and although this was better than nothing it hardly provided them both with food, and certainly there was nothing left for clothes and furniture. Sophie still used her savings to buy additional necessities, but, convinced that she must find a job to supplement their finances, started to apply for teaching posts in private schools outside London. She was eventually offered a temporary post as a governess at Felixstowe; and so, after only four months, Sophie left London. The psychological effect of these first four months might have destroyed the endeavour of many men, but it is interesting to see how with Sophie temporarily removed to Felixstowe, Gaudier, who had been working dejectedly in his study of art, redirected his energies and concentrated all his efforts on it.

We are completely dependent on the correspondence between Gaudier and Sophie during the rest of 1911 for most of our knowledge of the events which influenced his artistic development.

It has already been stated that Gaudier was involved in an artistic exploration of the museums and libraries of London almost as soon as he arrived, but, until 5 April, we have no record of the kind of activities in which he had been engaged. Ezra Pound's writings are therefore particularly useful:

'Another notebook, beginning 5 April 1911, contains notes on pigment, academic studies of muscles, sketches from Goya, a consideration of "La Question Juive", containing the statements that "Un *Juif* a tort d'abord parceque *Juif* c'est un être pratiquant une religion *absurde*", and that Christ's reform was "contre le nationalism".'

The sketchbook also contains what might be considered the germ of his first 'Vortex'; it shows him already considering the dominant characteristics of the different periods of sculpture, with an objection to Egypt because 'Mysticisms nuit à la vraie sensation d'art. S'est servie de la sculpture comme d'un instrument pour élever des colosses de granit, Temoins de sa philosophie.'

The most interesting note in the book is his revolt from 'Michel Ange 20 April 1911' as follows:

'dessiner dans les plans majeurs les masses principales
    „   „   „   masses „   „   plans mineurs
    „   „   „   plans mineurs „   masses   „

et rendre fermes ces masses mineures par l'étude correcte et vraie de tous leurs plans.

'Je crois que cette manière de travailler conduit à un détail magnifiquement véridique mai toujours contenu dans un ensemble imposant, faisant pour ainsi dire cet ensemble même.

'La ligne est une chose purement imaginative, elle ne vient dans le dessin que pour contenir les plans de la masse, recevant la lumière et créant l'ombre, les plans convoient le seule sensation artistique et la ligne ne leur sert que de cadre. L'artiste recherchant la pureté de la ligne et y adjustant les plans erre, il ajuste un tableau à un certain cadre et non un cadre à un certain tableau, c'est pourquoi je hais Ingres, Flaxman et les préraphaélites, et tous les sculpteurs modernes à l'exception de Dalou, Carpeaux, Rodin, Bourdelle et quelques autres.'[26]

These two statements were the first real assertions by Gaudier that revealed any positive development in his attitudes towards drawing and sculpture. The latter supports other evidence which suggests that he had ignored insurmountable problems of his day-to-day existence and was fully involved in studying art every minute of his free time. His first letter home after his arrival in London coincides with the departure of Sophie for Felixstowe. This very long letter, discussing politics, women and art,[27] confirms that with her departure came a release and consequent revitalized enthusiasm. Gaudier's corespondence with Sophie on the other hand, was cautous, 'to keep up appearances'; each letter begins and concludes with sentimental endearments, which, in all but a few examples, had little to do with the main content of his writing, which excitedly told of his enthusiasm and frustrations in 'finding himself' in his art.[28]

His first letter to Sophie, typical of this double image, began,

My dearest mother,
    I expect you are much better now, Pik [Gaudier's

nickname] is as well, he was very miserable yesterday but he slept for hours the night you left — and last night too,

and then continued:

I did not go to the park, but to the museum instead and I have found some wonderful casts of a study of a slave by Michelangelo[29]. . . . Now to our own business. I have received a reply this morning to the advertisement of last week, they have sent me patterns similar to drawings, 'calicots', and they have asked me to send some examples of my work and if it is suitable they will give me a commission. I am going to disobey Mamus again, I will work all this afternoon and this evening as well as all day tomorrow.[30]

This letter was continued and developed the next day when he wrote to Sophie again; here his enthusiasms were given true exposure and he was obviously feeling a real involvement and satisfaction in his discoveries. A statement early in the letter about being bored can hardly mean that he had time on his hands, but probably referred to his work as a translating secretary with Wulfsberg, which he obviously found as repetitive and uninteresting as his earlier employment in Paris.

I have continued with the study of the forms and arrangements of Michelangelo's 'famous planes', but without finding any more than I did two days ago. I only reaffirmed that what I had previously seen was true. I always have about ten 'kids' around me when I am drawing the slaves. They are obviously astonished at my behaviour, because I write as much as I draw; I look for a long time at that which I wish to understand. I work in a style which intrigues them a great deal, because I do not draw; instead of drawing the figure straight away as they are used to seeing everyone else do, I draw square boxes altering the size, one for each plane, and then suddenly by drawing a few lines between the boxes they can see the statue appear. They look at me with suspicion — with respect, I don't know whether it is because they find me so strict, or because of the drawing itself; whatever it is they amuse me. I think perhaps it is the drawing which is at the root of it, for men respect and revere or rather fear that which they cannot understand and consequently astonishes them.[31]

Replying to a letter from Sophie at this time he again started the letter with affection, 'Very beautiful most beloved Zofia,' but having made an endearing introduction, continued by explaining he was studying the Old Masters to keep silly romantic notions out of his mind because they upset him. They upset him so much that he could not make up his mind where to go when he went out to study: the Tate Gallery, Kew Gardens or the Berkshire countryside. This letter really reveals his dilemma. Sophie wanted him as her 'fils adoptif', Gaudier needed her encouragement and interest as comfort to his isolation, but not for his art. In fact at this time Sophie was a prohibiting influence on his creativity; but he subjected himself to her demands by recognizable tokens in letters and by signing his work with their two names, Gaudier Brzeska.

Another example which illustrates the obvious release he felt with the departure of Sophie, is that in spite of many months of no correspondence between them he wrote again to Kitty. Kitty Smith's later interpretation of the breakdown in their correspondence between this letter of 1911 and 1914 was, 'probably because we had nothing in common (I not being the least intelligent and with no knowledge of art) he found the correspondence rather boring.'[32] The main difference between this letter to Kitty and the letter to Sophie is its direct honesty of intention:

I am glad to live here because of the museum and libraries — I go out to the country every week to cheer up the ideas and get bodily strength as well. Friends? I have none yet — I am very difficult now about them — they must be rare sorts of men, having the same needs as I have, whom I can understand and who can understand me — Say to yourself that I am a funny specimen of mankind, a fanatic, or whatever you may think, but before everything a very stern boy always thinking of clay, stone, chisels and bodies to sculpt and considering everything else as second-rate matter.[33]

All the letters written in the first four months in London are important in that they firmly establish a pattern which can be followed throughout the rest of Gaudier's life; but he did not again simultaneously turn to Kitty and his parents until he faced similar difficulties some years later. Between January and April Sophie established a unique relationship with Gaudier and had it not been for the break caused by her absence in April 1911 it is doubtful if Gaudier could have survived the pressures of their coexistence.

The next letter which we know of confirms this earlier sense of freedom and establishes new values which recur later, particularly that of 'vitality'. Although the opening to the letter contains criticism of her wanting to find a permanent teaching post outside London, this again was only Gaudier writing what Sophie wanted to read. The change of content in his letter is almost defiant. 'Now, let's talk about art.'[34] The correspondence of this period is therefore important in understanding how his sculpture emerged in later years. During these months he adopted and rejected many ideas; these he expounded to Sophie because there was no one else, no teacher, no authority. Unfortunately, though, Sophie also had a claustrophobic effect on him, and the problem of how to appease her was such that he did not really know whether his life would be easier if she were living with him in London instead of his writing a succession of fanciful sentiments to keep her quiet. It is noticeable also that, in spite of Sophie, his letters have a

growing strength of conviction; they are more assertive particularly where he writes about his own drawing and its importance to him. The following letter, both in its length and its assertion, shows how his attitudes were developing and it is in his letter writings of this period that he continued to resolve his own thinking.

I am very sad also about Delannoy's death.[35] I am very fond of his style of drawing; it was strong and that explains why his later work was not as good as the earlier drawings, it's because the poor devil was ill. I have religiously kept close to the original likeness;[36] it's a bit weak but all the same one can see his character, it must be the reproduction in black of a coloured original which makes it weak. You see, Mamus, I'm right again: that a fine and great artist must also be a simple, good and handsome man. I will never give up this philosophy and you can say what you like about it being presumptuous to judge a character by a face; contrary to the proverb, one cannot judge a man by his appearance. . . . Now about statues, best of all I like *Jean*, I admire the *Slave* for its sheer size, its heroism, its astonishing creative energy, *Victory* because its sensuous poetry pleases me, but I understand neither one nor the other even though I often make out I do. I can't look at them for long without getting tired; with the exception of Rodin's *John the Baptist*, which would hold me for days on end. . . . In my opinion the *St Jean* is more beautiful than the *Venus*, for I understand beauty in a different way to Phidias. It is a beggar who walks, who stops to chat and gesticulate — it belongs to my own time, is in my speech, is in my epoch, has a twentieth-century workman's body, just as I see it and know it; to summarize: it's a lovely statue. I like it better than the others because I believe that art should be of the present day; discovered in the present and not in the past.

I remain aloof to anyone who reproaches me for not having seen the Greeks. Sir, I would say, if you had made me then, I would have been able to see them; but it would be my greatest shame if anyone accused me of not being able to see what was around me. . . . If there are only beggars today then let us only sculpt beggars; if we no longer have subjects suitable for gigantic paintings, then let us not paint gigantic paintings, so that our successors will not be able to accuse us of having been false in our time. Since I believe in the eternity of life on this earth and in the breaking up of life's forces to be renewed again, I think it is deceitful to lie about this. I am as much a part of the past as of the future, I respect both, but the latter is more important. Our imagination helps us to understand the present, not to create things. In Pik's creative thinking it is utterly forbidden to express anything other than that which is real, that, little Mamus, is what makes the greatness of Phidias, of Michelangelo, they did not represent the Egyptians or Gauls but their contemporaries. Rodin will be as big a man for the twentieth century as Michelangelo is for the sixteenth — but you must not compare one with the other — do you see Mamuska?[37]

Gaudier's study of Rodin had obviously given him confidence in discussing his own work, but to counterbalance his growing assurance Sophie continued to upset him with paradoxes about art. His previous letter was perhaps the strongest statement he had made about his beliefs up to this time, and, challenged by Sophie, it was followed by another, extracts from which illustrate his developing ideas.

You are a little joker — what self-contradictory statements you try to get me to believe.

The true artist neither wants to be, nor is aware of being one. That is the equivalent to saying that Michel-Ange, a great artist, never knew that he was a better sculptor than Desid[erio] da Settignano or Giovanni da Bologna, who were his contemporaries, and that he created the slaves 'without being aware of it'; and this after he had spent years making studies so that he could get as much life and movement into them as possible and as much texture in the modelling. . . . The truth is, that a great artist is conscious of his own talents and abilities otherwise he wouldn't see his faults and so wouldn't be able to improve.

The first thing is: That sculpture is composed of the placing of planes according to a rhythm. That Literature is composed of the placing of stories according to a rhythm. That music is composed of the placing of sounds according to a rhythm, and that deviation from any one of these rules is not permitted, that they are precisely confined and limited and that any infringement by one or other is a mistake in taste and understanding.[38]

Although this letter is concluded in the usual tones of endearment, it was not the kind of letter to please Sophie. The only reason he may have felt able to write in such a way was perhaps because he had offered to go down and see her for a few days at the end of the month. It did little to cool her temper and her reply was filled with abuse. Obviously aware of the effect his letters were having, Gaudier was content to continue his criticism of Sophie's attitudes. It is quite evident that these letters had become as important to him for sounding out and expressing his ideas as those written earlier to Dr Uhlemayr and his father, the only difference being that he was now assimilating his own ideas. Rodin's sculpture was still of considerable significance to him and in his next letter he again used statements by Rodin to support his arguments. He must have been overjoyed with chapters such as, 'Movement in Art', from Rodin's book, L'Art, which expressed in his own language ideas which he had himself been searching to express; consequently, when he quoted Rodin to Sophie, the context was sometimes changed as he 'adopted' the master for himself. The point which em-

erges from these letters more strongly than any other is that his own resolve to make something of art was now truly determined. 'I am absolutely certain that what I feel is really "true".' Sculpture was certainly of more importance to him at this time than any other means of expression, but his interest in it was still chiefly theoretical:

I must impress on you once again the mathematical side of sculpture. Here is a cube — it is beautiful because it has light and shade — now here are a collection of cubes which give me great satisfaction — I can inscribe within them the body of a woman. It is not beautiful because it's a woman of such and such a kind but because it catches the light in a certain way. If you want to dream in front of it so much the better, but under no circumstances must you accuse the sculptor primarily of having wished to express vice or virtue. His concern is to make a beautiful statue, from a material point of view.[39]

This extract from a long letter, together with a much shorter one written two days later, represents the peak of Gaudier's enthusiasm for Rodin during 1911. Obviously, he was once again feeling less depressed with life and, as was his usual manner when in good spirits, he had written to his parents, to Dr Uhlemayr, and agreed to visit Felixstowe to see Sophie. His letter to Dr Uhlemayr told him how happy he was, but hinted at some of the disillusion he obviously felt, by stating 'how sorry I am that England which was so beautiful should be owned by a people so ugly.'[40] The visit to see Sophie made him determined to persuade her to return to London, and it was eventually decided that she should stay at Burnham until the end of August, by which time Gaudier would have found suitable new rooms in London. This decision was disastrous for both of them and for the next six months a great deal of their time and energy was again spent solely in the struggle to exist. Little documentation, notebooks or sketches remain from between August and December, and Gaudier obviously did not even have the inclination to continue earlier correspondence. The preoccupying problem was to find accommodation in London which they could afford, since that which they did find was so often filthy and dilapidated that within a few weeks of taking it Sophie insisted on moving. They moved all their possessions at least four times, lastly to 45 Paulton's Square, Chelsea. In addition to their poverty there is little evidence that, after six months, they knew anyone in London to whom they could turn for help. There were no friends to whom Gaudier could talk about art, and consequently he was still dependent on his own reading and drawing, and visits to museums and galleries, for all the stimulation for his work. Not surprisingly, he seems to lose momentum during these later months, except that he was busily engaged producing a variety of posters, anticipating that these would make his art financially successful. Only a few of these drawings remain today and it is easy to see from their size why they did not appeal to publicity agents. Many of them have either Sophie as their subject-matter, or people whom Gaudier saw and sketched outside in the street. Often these drawings are satirical and reflect his depressed mood and feeling of isolation.

Significantly, the isolation was broken towards the end of the year by two events. Firstly, Gaudier and Sophie saw a man outside the National Gallery to whom they were both attracted, but neither dared approach. On meeting the same man a few days later Gaudier was again reluctant to approach him, but Sophie did, asked him if he spoke French or Polish, rapidly explained her dislike of the English, and invited him to meet Henri her brother, who was a sculptor. As a result of this introduction, after nearly a year in London, Arrigo Levasti, an Italian from Verona, became their first friend.[41] Secondly, the week before Christmas, Gaudier had a pay increase to £9 per month and a £5 Christmas bonus; this, together with his happiness over his new friend, broke the continuous monotony of his depression, and on 28 December a once more jubilant Gaudier wrote to his sister Renée. The letter contained money for a birthday present and instructions on how to spend it 'wisely' buying paints and a drawing book. This letter does not really reflect the desperate isolation Gaudier felt during the last twelve months. It does, however, reveal his undaunted will to succeed against seemingly insuperable odds. The brief friendship of Arrigo Levasti must have given him new confidence to find friends, because very early in the new year he made approaches in other directions.

NOTES:
1. Letter from Gaudier's father. 13.12.1928. Private collection. Unpublished.
2. Letter from Gaudier's father. 25.11.1928. Private collection. Unpublished.
3. Letter from Gaudier's father. 25.11.1928. Private collection. Unpublished.
4. Letter from M. Gallonedez. 18.11.1928. Private collection. Unpublished.
5. Kitty Smith. B.B.C. Broadcast. 19.5.1965.
6. Letter to H. S. Ede. 1930. Kettle's Yard. Cambridge University.
7. Letter from Alfred Hazell. Private collection. Unpublished.
8. Sketchbooks. Kettle's Yard, Cambridge University and Musée National d'Art Moderne, Paris.
9. Sketchbooks. Kettle's Yard, Cambridge University and Musée National d'Art Moderne, Paris.
10. Letter to Gaudier's parents. 20.4.1909. Kettle's Yard, Cambridge University.
11. Sketchbook. Musée National d'Art Moderne, Paris.
12. Letter from Dr Uhlemayr. 25.3.1929. Private collection. Unpublished.
13. Letter to Kitty Smith. 31.8.1909. Private collection. Unpublished.
14. Letter to Dr Uhlemayr. 10.10.1909.
15. Letter to Dr Uhlemayr. 1.1.1910.
16. Letter. Pound,1, p. 41.
17. Pound, 1, p. 41.
18. Letter to Dr Uhlemayr. 5.3.1910. Private collection.
19. Letter to Kitty Smith. 22.8.1910. Private collection. Unpublished.
20. Letter to Kitty Smith. 26.3.1910. Private collection. Unpublished.
21. Letter to Kitty Smith. 2.4.1910. Private collection. Unpublished.
22. Letter to Dr Uhlemayr. 24.5.1910. Private collection. Part published.
23. Letter to Dr Uhlemayr. 4.10.1910. Major part of this letter remains unpublished.
24. This sculpture appears in Gaudier's original List of Works. Kettle's Yard, Cambridge University.
25. Lengthy correspondence and documentation give intimate details of this family disaster. Private collection.
26. Pound, 1, pp. 42–3.
27. Letter to Gaudier's parents. 25.2.1911. Copy Musée National d'Art Moderne, Paris. Whereabouts of original not known.
28. Author's interpretation. From J. A. Dickinson & Son, to whom Gaudier had applied for work.
29. Author's interpretation of abbreviation.
30. Letter to Sophie. 22.4.1911. Essex University Library.
31. Letter to Sophie. 23.4.1911. Essex University Library.
32. Letter from Kitty Smith. 25.8.1932. Private collection. Unpublished.
33. Letter to Kitty Smith. 21.4.1911. Private collection. Unpublished.
34. Letter to Sophie. 13.5.1911. Essex University Library. Part published: Ede, 1, p. 57.
35. Delannoy, Aristide. Died 5.5.1911.
36. Referring to a sketch included in original letter. Present whereabouts of original not known.
37. Letter to Sophie. 19.5.1911. Essex University Library. Full text unpublished.
38. Letter ? Gaudier to Sophie. Sunday, 5.1911. Essex University Library. Part published.
39. Letter to Sophie. 3.6.1911. Extracts from Essex University Library. Part previously published: Ede, 1, p. 84.
40. Letter to Dr Uhlemayr. 12.6.1911. Summary copy Musée National d'Art Moderne, Paris.
41. Extract from Sophie's diary. Essex University Library.

2

A search for identity

1911 *to* 1912

As a result of reading an article in the January issue of the *English Review* entitled 'The Puritan and the Theatre', Gaudier wrote to Haldane Macfall:

Your essay in this month's number of the *English Review* has awoken in me a craving to make your acquaintance. It is very hard to find here someone who looks at life in the broader sense — in a manner freed from all prejudice and who dares say that Art is a vital need — I came to London a year ago and though I have not missed one single opportunity to come near to anybody whom I thought would be worth knowing I have not so far succeeded. You are well able to understand the kind of loneliness and self disgust that has overcome me.[1]

Macfall invited Gaudier to visit his home and immediately offered to help him by suggesting possibilities for selling his work, and encouraging him to feel that together they would soon make it possible for him to earn his living as an artist. On this first visit he also met two of Macfall's friends, Messrs Hardinge and Allfree,[2] and he was so encouraged by their optimism about his future success that he invited them to visit his apartment the next day to see his work. Events moved so rapidly in fact that on 15 January he wrote to Macfall telling him it was far too early yet to think of a one-man exhibition of his work since it still showed too much foreign influence![3] Although aware of 'foreign influence' this did not deter him from studying sculpture; in fact he was inspired to work harder. He kept in close contact with Macfall, telling him of his latest enthusiasm. 'I am off to the British Museum this afternoon — I profit always doubly there for not only do I enjoy, at the highest degree, the marvellous sculptures of the ancients, but I find very good models in the visitors,

not a very great lot of them are characteristically interesting, but I am at leisure to study movement undisturbed.[4]

This interest in 'ancient sculpture', together with a 'Rodin-influenced' interest in the moving figure, is a significant point in his development, since Gaudier had assured Macfall that he would start his own sculpture in February. In addition to studying he was also trying to sell his designs for posters and book jackets to a Mr Martin, a friend of Macfall's, but with little success. The enthusiasm with which Macfall encouraged Gaudier was perhaps more important than the sale of the posters, since it made him believe in his own ability. Macfall encouraged him to move towards sculpture, and kept him so busy that 'he had little time to concern himself with his lack of financial resources, the squalid nature of his lodgings, or with Sophie'.[5] By the second week in February (with Macfall's help), Gaudier had succeeded in acquiring further useful contacts. Amongst these was Holbrook Jackson, who suggested that he should have his portrait modelled,[6] and Leman Hare, who wanted him to make a statuette of Maria Carmi as the Madonna at Olympia (No. 3).[7] This first commission fired his enthusiasm, particularly since Mrs Hare had said that Lord Northcliffe had asked to be 'put down for £50'.[8]

Gaudier set to work eagerly on the clay model of the figure; he worked in the evenings and at the weekend and by 26 February had completed the model and had made a plaster mould from it. He was ill-equipped to handle the clay in the two small rooms at his apartment, but even less well equipped to handle plaster which smothered everything, and infuriated Sophie. The two casts of Maria Carmi were completed, one for Lord Northcliffe and one for Leman Hare. Lord Northcliffe did not like his and gave Leman Hare only £5 to pay to Gaudier. This was his first three-dimensional piece of work, apart from an early portrait bust of his father and it may be regarded as his first serious sculpture.

The main reasons for Gaudier's sudden involvement in sculpture can thus be attributed to Macfall. The following extract from a letter gives an interesting insight into his feelings at this time. The problems with the Carmi statue were technical and social, and he was still involved more in the theories behind art rather than the practical problems of their expression.

I am very sorry I have not seen you for such a long time but that statuette has given me such a lot of trouble that I have hardly been able to take a few hours' rest a day. The mould is finished and I trust to cast it tonight. That plaster business puts my rooms into such a state of filth that it is simply disgusting to look at and never more will I undertake getting such a thing ready in so short a space of time.

I had an invitation from Major Smythies to go to his house last night and I met Simpson and Fraser there. I was disappointed to learn that you had not been able to come. He has a Burmese seal, which you doubtless know — the tiger biting the sun, with very terrific movement and diabolism, qualities which appeal to me much.

Lately I have been digesting all the observations I have made for a year or so and drawn some marks in the way I mean to sculpt them: painted so as to give the absolute characteristical complexion modified by the occasional expression but just as simple and bright as can be — I use for that the optic mixing of the colours — putting them in pure pigments side by side so as to give the resulting tone — I will fix some of them and bring them for you to see on the evening of Wednesday the 28th if convenient.[9]

Through Macfall's generosity, Gaudier continued to meet new friends. Macfall has written:

Of all the brilliant little group of writers and artists and art-lovers who were wont to take possession of our flat of a Wednesday evening — the early doomed Henri Gaudier; Enid Bagnold, since come to repute with her verses; Miss Bieber, an artistic and handsome girl, like the others who happened to be a particularly beautiful bevy; Leith Ross and his charming and accomplished wife; Dolly Tylden, who afterwards married the son of Sir William Crundall the mayor of Dover; Henry Hardinge, who was writing plays and came to success with *Carnival*; my old comrade Major Raymond Smythies; and the others — Lovat was the life and soul. I can see them all sitting about the rooms, on chair or sofa or carpet, caricaturing one another. Enid Bagnold, a very beautiful girl, daughter of Colonel Bagnold of the Sappers, and now married to Sir Roderick Jones, made some witty caricatures of Lovat and of Gaudier; and I can hear the laughter that came when Lovat, who wore his dark hair somewhat long, arose after some tomfoolery, and standing upon his massive six foot

and more, with his dark hair rumpled about his eyes, fired off some ridiculous sally, whereupon Enid Bagnold withered him with 'Lovat, do get some hairpins and be reasonable!' Indeed, Lovat's mass of dark locks and the three or reputed five ridiculous hairs on Gaudier's chin that Lovat libellously called Gaudier's beard, were the theme of many a caricature.[10]

The importance of these conversations cannot be over-emphasized. As has already been noted Gaudier thrived on intellectual discussion and argument and his delight with the opportunities presented by the company at Macfall's house knew no bounds. Macfall raised his hopes to such an extent that he often went back to Sophie after such visits talking of giving up his work as a clerk altogether. Not surprisingly the second sculpture Gaudier produced bore little resemblance to the first except in subject-matter. Maria Carmi had played the part of the nun in *The Miracle* and his second sculpture, entitled *Maternity* (No. 02), is obviously derivative from religious statuary and intended to appeal particularly to Mrs Hare. She enthused over the work and wished to purchase it immediately it was completed.

When remembering this sale in her diary Sophie recalled Gaudier saying, 'Oh, do take it as a present if it pleases you.'[11] Its casting had cost him twenty-five shillings, but nothing would have induced him to mention this, and when Mrs Hare offered him £3, he felt rich indeed. The Hares obviously wanted to help Gaudier and if it had not been for Sophie's untruthful minimizing of their financial and domestic problems it is likely that they would have helped them much more. On the completion of these two sculptures, Major Smythies showed further interest in his portrait being modelled and was as anxious as Macfall that Gaudier should make a start. Gaudier was too inexperienced to handle more than one sculpture at a time. He was without a personal style and was still desperately searching for a preferred medium.

This was further exemplified by the muddle which developed when Macfall introduced him to R. Macfarlane Cocks,[12] who was so enthusiastic about Gaudier's future that he commissioned three pieces of work to be sent to him when completed and wrote out a cheque for £30 in payment. The three sculptures which Gaudier sent were all in terracotta: *Pot à fleurs*, *Deux demi-statuettes* and *Plâteau*.[13] *Pot à fleurs* was broken when Mr Cocks moved house in 1919 and little else is known about it except that it had on its four sides heads modelled in bas-relief. The other two sculptures do not seem to have impressed either Cocks or Macfall, who, in his letter to Brodzky, suggested that because they were so poor Gaudier missed the opportunity of acquiring a wealthy patron.[14]

Gaudier's lack of respect and arrogance towards patrons and contacts whom he hardly knew seems to be a characteristic which shows itself for the first time during the early months of 1912. Lovat Fraser tolerated much of this kind of abuse from Gaudier, who jibed and attacked Lovat's elegance and dandy figure. Instead of allowing this to disrupt his support and encouragement, Lovat continued to visit Gaudier with his friends and, in return for financial assistance in purchasing his materials, Gaudier made a number of tiles and masks, direct copies of primitive designs, and also decorated with gaudy colours the staircase and woodwork in Fraser's studio. The largest mask (No. 4), which to date is the only one known to survive, stemmed in its concept from the earlier study of the primitive and reflected some of the ideas discussed in earlier letters. The mask was painted in crude bright colours and gilded on parts of the face. It is another example of a work which had little relationship with previous sculpture apart from surface colour, but was part of his positive search for a medium and a style.

In spite of the apparent inconsistency in his sculpture Gaudier continued to draw. These drawings and early pastels were still inquisitive, and retain even today a vitality and confidence which was not present in his modelling. In offering one of the drawings of this period to the British Museum Lovat Fraser wrote:

'It is almost, I think, the only survivor of a whole host of notebooks that he filled with drawings of Whitechapel types, that he used to make in his lunch hour.'[15] There is, however, a positive link between the portrait drawings of this period and the portraits in clay. Gaudier merely extended his interpretation to three dimensions. Consequently, in spite of the derogatory remarks he made to Sophie about his sitters, namely Haldane Macfall and Major Smythies, here was a natural development from his draw-

This bust of Enid Bagnold is of the same period as the portrait head of Major Smythies (No. 5). Clay modelling provided Gaudier with an immediate and inexpensive material, into which he would rapidly translate his searchings for a sculptural style. The portrait explores some of the possibilities of simplified form and like the Major Smythies portrait is an exploratory exercise for the more expressive portraits which were to follow. The bust appears in Gaudier's List of Works: *'larger than life size', and is dated 1912.*

ing of the human head into three dimensions. Macfall's account of his visit to Gaudier's apartment to have his head modelled gives an interesting insight, which suggests that much of Gaudier's behaviour was in fact showmanship, and echoes of Rodin's ideas, rather than the behaviour of a serious sculptor: 'He had said that he didn't require his sitters to sit, and indeed liked them to walk about; but Zosik noticed that it was a great relief to him when Macfall said he would prefer to sit down.'

The portraits of Smythies and Macfall (Nos 5, 6) are very reminiscent of some aspects of Rodin's bust of Clemenceau and show that Gaudier had not only a control in his handling of the clay but, particularly in the portrait of Smythies, even adopted techniques of modelling as practised by Rodin.

During this time Macfall was still encouraging to Gaudier, in fact pressing him to exhibit his work. Replying, Gaudier wrote: 'I have reflected upon it and I find it is much wiser to wait till next autumn before having a show — I will have much more then — I have just finished a vase and am portraying Miss Bagnold next Sunday 12th inst.'[16]

The dismissal of the idea for an exhibition was obviously sensible, but although Gaudier did not break off contact with Macfall completely their relationship gradually cooled from this point onwards. Gaudier had made a number of other contacts during his friendship with Macfall and some of these now occupied more of his time. Amongst his new friends was Enid Bagnold, and since Gaudier was now interested in portrait heads he asked Enid Bagnold if he could make a bust of her. The portrait head he created is no more significant than those of Macfall and Smythies, but it is more important in emphasizing a recurring pattern of portrait busts which continued throughout the next two years.

It is true to say, at this point, that Gaudier learnt best and most effectively through a process of elimination. Certainly his drawing improved through progressive stages of refinement and these clay portrait busts must be regarded as solid groundwork for the sculpture which was to follow, while at the same time each one is a limited progressive development in its own right.

The next important stage in Gaudier's sculptural development was also as a result of his meeting new friends, this time Jacob Epstein. A record of Gaudier's first meeting with Epstein is contained in a letter to Dr Uhlemayr:

A Russian sculptor Jacob Epstein also works here — he has just finished a tomb (sarcophagus) for Oscar Wilde in Paris.[17] The thing will be erected at the Père Lachaise cemetery next July. I saw it in the studio last Sunday — Oscar Wilde is flying slowly into space, his eyes shut. The whole work is treated — strongly, filled with insuperable movement and delicate feeling, in the expression and the medium — a piece of sculpture which will live for ever, only the total effect seems to be too small.

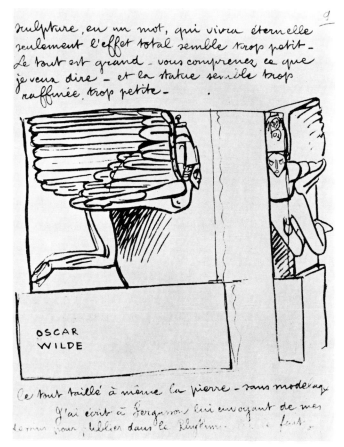

sculpture, en un mot, qui vivra éternelle -
seulement l'effet total semble trop petit -
Le tout est grand - vous comprenez ce que
je veux dire - et la statue semble trop
raffinée, trop petite -

OSCAR
WILDE

Ce tout taillé à même la pierre - sans modelage
J'ai écrit à Fergusson lui envoyant de mes ...

Letter from Henri Gaudier with a sketch of Epstein's tomb of Oscar Wilde

Gaudier would certainly have been impressed by Epstein and judging by the sketch enclosed in this letter to Uhlemayr he made a close study of the Oscar Wilde sarcophagus.

At a later date Epstein dismissed Gaudier's first visit with indifference. 'He took to carving after admiring work he saw in my studio.'[18]

This remark is far more likely to be true than the elaborate but delightful fantasy told by Brodzky, attributed to Frank Harris, who said that on meeting Epstein, Gaudier was asked by him, 'Do . . . you cut direct . . . in stone?' 'Most certainly,' said Gaudier, who had never yet done anything of the sort. 'That's right,' said Epstein, 'I will come round to your place on Sunday.' So Gaudier at once went out, got three small stone blocks and by working more or less night and day had something ready by Sunday.[19]

The significance of his meeting with Epstein was that here was a real sculptor, a foreigner earning a living in London by being an artist; Gaudier admired this more than anything else. He was impressed by the sculpture and may

well have started stone carving as a result of this visit to Epstein's studio, but, whatever he produced, he thought it of so little importance that when, in 1914, he made out a list of the works he had completed,[20] he did not include any stone carving for this period. In early summer Epstein returned to Paris where his notoriety as a result of the Wilde tomb endeared him to artists of the avant-garde movement; consequently his particular influence on Gaudier at this time was short.

Macfall, meanwhile, continued to provide Gaudier with interested clients and, as a result of one of these introductions, Gaudier met Mr Walter Benington, a portrait photographer, thinking that he wanted a portrait bust and was prepared to pay £30 for it. As with many of Macfall's other bright ideas this was never mentioned by Benington to Gaudier, but at Macfall's instigation Benington took a number of photographs of Gaudier's sculpture, which have remained in some instances the only references to his early work. Gaudier was obviously proud of the photographs because he sent some to his sister Renée.[21] Gaudier also used Macfall in other ways when he needed him, and sometimes tried to repair insults by giving him one or two drawings.[22]

In the summer, through Fergusson (a London publisher and artist), to whom Gaudier had hopefully sent some of his drawings, he and Sophie were introduced to Katherine Mansfield and Middleton Murry. From the start the relationship between them was one of confidences on either side. Murry had of course seen Gaudier's drawings and promised to publish them in the next issue of *Rhythm*;[23] and in return Gaudier started to model a portrait bust of Murry.[24] A complete account of this relationship is not relevant to Gaudier's sculptural development, but the effect of the loss in the late summer of these new-found friends did have repercussions in the relationship between Gaudier and Sophie. Briefly, the friendship broke down through Sophie's sudden enthusiasm for Murry and Mansfield's company. On 12 August[25] Murry and Mansfield had left London for Runcton Cottage, on the Selsey side of Chichester, Mansfield having offered to entertain both Sophie and Gaudier when the cottage there was redecorated. Sophie was eager to get out of the heat and noise of London and, not having heard from Mansfield by early September, sent Gaudier on a surprise visit to see if the cottage was finished.[26] Unfortunately, on approaching the cottage, Gaudier overheard Mansfield discussing with Murry her dread and concern at having to invite Sophie. Furious, Gaudier crept away unseen and immediately sent a dejected postcard to Sophie cursing *'les sales tigres'*.[27] So the friendship ended. With this disappointment they were both depressed, but once again it was Macfall who revitalized Gaudier's enthusiasm to work. Gaudier was this time commissioned by a Mr Lousada to create a portrait of *'de Bolm et Karsavina dans le ballet Russe' (No. 14)*.[28]

One consequence of Gaudier's friendship with Murry was that he met Edward Marsh. Murry had entertained Marsh and Rupert Brooke at Runcton Cottage early in September and on his return to London Marsh, anxious to meet Gaudier, invited him to dinner to look at his pictures. The reply to Marsh reveals an interesting insight into Gaudier's suspicion of authority, which is certainly a direct reflection of the circumstances which compelled him to leave France: 'Your envelope bearing the Admiralty Seal gave me a sort of fright — I had a vague idea I was going to be arrested for some reason or other.'[29]

In spite of new friendships and the commissions from clients such as Lousada, Sophie was very pessimistic about the future. The summer heat and the noise in their apartment had strained her nerves, and the disappointment over Runcton Cottage aggravated her pessimism still further. In a fit of temper and frustration Sophie left London for the country and Gaudier was once more alone in London. Her departure had a similar immediate effect on Gaudier as previously; he had more time to work on his sculpture, more time to think, and when writing to Sophie the opportunity to consolidate his ideas in his letters. The difficulties of the relationship between Sophie and Gaudier can be said to have hindered his sculptural development in this important year and it is not surprising, in the light of what he had produced by the time Sophie left London, to find in a letter he wrote to her, that he expounds a belief that his work is 'in the moment'.

Your letter upset me a great deal. . . . From one end to the other you do everything you can to find fault with me . . . I look at things a great deal and I do a lot of drawing so that I can see how things differ, inter-relate and clash with each other. I am never certain that what I say or think is true, and even less certain that what I have said or thought is true and that I am able to sacrifice some new ideas which are completely different from those I had yesterday just because they had the good fortune to come into my head and whilst there I relentlessly advocated them. Do you realize that I have to be in a filthy office all day and that every minute I am subjected to torturous desires to be cutting stone, painting walls and casting statues? You always seem to forget this and it's very rude of you. I only know stupid people but through them may be able to extricate myself from this hell of shipbroking etc. and of course I am not going to change course in search of some vain glory because my pride has been hurt. I am of the same opinion as Machiavelli that when you want to attain an objective you must use every means available, for when everything is considered and analysed, the misery I put up with at work is far greater than the insignificant troubles of the soul, mind and understanding which I put up with in my dealings with these pigs that I know. . . . Since you are so determined to be alone, stay alone, I will, for my part, manage as best I can.[30]

The conclusion to this letter also contained abusive comments about Lovat Fraser, who earlier had provided him with tickets for free outings to the zoo, in return for the plaster mask. 'Can you let me have some more zoo tickets . . . the mask will be ready in middle January, that is: painted ready to hang.'[31] Quite clearly Gaudier was still far less concerned to accommodate these friends than he should have been. They had been used by him and had served their purpose for the time being, and as soon as one of them did anything of which Gaudier disapproved he was cutting in his criticism and 'furiously abusive of most of those with whom he came in contact'.[32] This could be excused but it is surprising since in most instances Gaudier was critical of those who had helped him the most. He was entirely involved with himself and with a conscious selfish determination — not only to succeed but to climb above those who surrounded him, often those on whom he depended. He explained his awareness of his own position in a letter to Sophie.

I regret many things that I have said and done, you must realize, Zosik, that I have only just opened my eyes to the world and I am dazzled. My feelings are not altogether aligned with my reason, my words fail to express exactly what I want to say. My understanding is scanty, and the primitive qualities in my nature take the upper hand.

About my ideas on art, I modify them continually and I'm very pleased to do it. If I allowed myself to remain with a fixed idea, I would develop mannerisms and ruin my whole development. From what I can put together at the moment, I believe that art is the interpretation of emotion, and consequently of the idea. I recognize that the discipline of the technique is necessary to this emotion, and at present I feel that the simpler the technique and more limited, the better the idea emerges. Now on the other

Postcard from Gaudier to Sophie, October 1912

hand I am aware that the more technique is limited the greater the danger is of adopting mannerisms, which negates all the emotion that we experience in front of nature. Again in this emotion I am conscious of three divisions:

The emotion of line produced by the rhythm of outlines and strokes.

Sculptural emotion produced by the balance of masses as they are revealed by light and shadow.

Pictorial emotion produced by the effect of the various coloured pigments.

These three technical emotions seem to be united by very strong ties, in a vast intellectual emotion, which I do not understand, and correspond to spiritual feelings of pleasure, suffering, sorrow, joy etc. etc. which I feel, and in that is the mystery of the whole thing. At one time I thought that it was sufficient to reproduce each form exactly — and then that it was only the light which was of importance and that if each tone of light was accurately recorded that which it lit would be accurate also. You will

Figure drawing, 1912

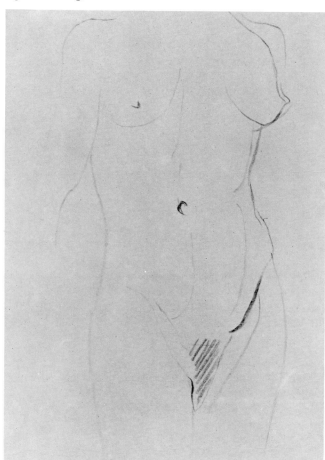

see for yourself it is best for me gradually to disentangle myself from these prejudices, to deny, so to speak, that which I thought instead of becoming stupidly swallowed up by it, so proving myself to be self-opinionated. To tell the truth I am sure of nothing since I have only just started to experience life to the full.

With the additional time he now had as a result of Sophie's absence, he explored other creative processes and ideas. Although this work must also be regarded as exploratory it provides an interesting insight into his search for an individually satisfactory means of expression (Nos 15–18). Gaudier's renewed interest in, and reference to Rodin, may have resulted from the publication of Rodin's *L'Art* in March 1911 and the subsequent interest which was aroused over the English translation by Mrs Romilly Fedden published in 1912. It is unlikely that he would have bothered to read the English version, but his renewed interest in Rodin at this time only helped him to find arguments to support and elucidate his own, sometimes confused, thinking.

Early November brought a renewed interest in Gaudier's work by Marsh. The re-establishment of this friendship was important since Marsh was another figurehead, like Macfall, at the centre of a group of aspiring young artists and writers. It was through this contact that Gaudier was to make a number of new friends in 1913. He was also feeling more confident about his work; Lousada was encouraging and promised, 'to try and have the bronze, *L'oiseau de Feu*, exhibited the following year in London'. Consequently Gaudier wrote to Macfall asking him if he would persuade Harris to 'put in a good word for him', and thereby not only get Lousada's sculpture exhibited but also Macfall's portrait bust.

Gaudier was also anticipating that Harris, whom he had met earlier through Lovat Fraser, would at last make arrangements for work to start on his portrait bust, which had been deferred many times. It was probably at about this date that Harris recalled meeting Gaudier in the British Museum, where Gaudier took him to see early Assyrian statues which he enthused over.[33]

Meanwhile Gaudier was drawing continuously both from life and at the zoo. Many of the drawings at this time show a change in interest of observation. This is revealed by the quantity of drawings which are concerned mainly with a profile image of a single line, and his prolific output. A single session often resulted in as many as 150 drawings. Working at such a speed, the style of the drawings, not surprisingly, became much more fluid.

Although Gaudier was still friendly with Fraser he had far more admiration for Epstein, who, having returned from Paris, was now working in London. In a letter to Sophie he described his first visit to see Epstein after his return and it is evident that he admired Epstein as a 'real sculptor'.

Self-portrait drawing, Christmas 1912

There's an enormous difference between little Epstein's place and the studios of 'Fraserkie' and others — little Epstein, all dirty and dusty, covered with plaster, sitting on the window-sill carving stone. He talked to me about his Oscar Wilde in Paris. When he arrived 'les worki' [testicles] were plastered over; then the Prefect of the Seine had the whole monument covered with straw as being altogether indecent. Epstein took off the straw and plaster, leaving Wilde with his 'couelles de taureau', which hung down a good half-metre, and thanks to the petition of some artists he got the better of the authorities. He showed me a little bronze, lovely, quite the best work of his I know, lively and sincere — a seated woman with her arms above her head; his founder is an Italian in Battersea called Fiorini whose charges are less than Parlanti. We smoked, discussed casting and stone as usual and then I went home.[34]

Epstein's return from Paris obviously brought with it new questions and new ideas; much of his time had been concerned with meeting, discussing and absorbing the new ideas of Paris, in particular the fascination for primitive art. Epstein had seen Modigliani every day for several months, he had purchased pieces of African sculpture that he could afford, and had met Picasso and Brancusi.[35] He was steeped in the revolutionary thinking of new movements in Paris led by artists and writers with whom he had lived, and it is not surprising to find Gaudier, having received a cold blast of truth from Epstein about the Paris movement, relating his own studies of the primitive in the British Museum to Epstein's thinking. He now had to decide his own position. In a letter to Sophie he discusses both these attitudes and another commission, which he had obtained from the brother of an artist friend, Ewart Wheeler.

He has recommended me to make ornaments for electric radiators, etc. In addition to this he is interested in sport and he has commissioned me to make two plaster statues, one of a wrestler, the other of a swimmer, which he will get one of his contacts to cut in bronze for him. Working in his office is the same wrestler that I have seen before, a magnificent young boy, strong and well built, square-shouldered, and I am going to see them wrestling in the evenings two or three times a week, which will give me the opportunity to make some good studies of them. . . . Regarding my visit to the British Museum; I took particular notice of all the primitive statues, negro, yellow, red and white races, Gothic and Greek, and I am pleased to say that I am now certain of one thing which had bothered me for a long time, whether the conventional forms in primitive sculpture which give enormous satisfaction, through severe happiness or expressive sorrow, and are produced by positive movement synthesized and directed only towards one end, do not reveal an understanding more at one with nature, in other words greater and with more understanding, than the modern sculpture of Pisani, Donatello, and up to Rodin and the French today. Men today are not satisfied with one movement as in primitive sculpture, the movement is now composed, is a sequence of other uninterrupted movements which in their turn can be sub-divided, and different parts of the body can move in opposing directions with varying intensity. Movement is the translation of life, and if art depicts life, then movement should be an integral part of art since we are only aware of life because it moves.[36]

Much of this letter contains Gaudier's attempt to differentiate between Rodin's attitudes to art and those ideas which he understood from Epstein as being explored in Paris. This is in fact the first real questioning by Gaudier of Rodin's concepts; he has previously been able to find arguments to counterbalance Rodin's attitudes about movement, and similarly now cannot accept all the concepts, as expounded by Epstein, of primitive sculpture. He sees sculpture as composed of a sequence of movements in opposing directions, with varying intensity. His struggles with these ideas, together with an increasing feeling of self-assurance, must have encouraged him to look for a studio, since he was now seriously considering giving up his job to work solely on his sculpture.[37] Meanwhile plans went ahead for Gaudier to submit ideas for some car mascots, and arrangements were made for him to visit St Bride's School, where two brothers named Bacon posed for him. Gaudier was wildly enthusiastic with this opportunity, and wrote and told Sophie of his enthusiasm and included sketches of the wrestling.[38] Unfortunately, his enthusiasm, perhaps aspiring towards making a sculpture comparable to Epstein, carried him beyond reason. Recalling this incident one of the brothers later wrote: 'Gaudier came to St Bride's School and sketched us. The statuettes Wheeler wanted were never done, you see he wanted something 9" or 12" high and Gaudier did something in plaster of 2 or 3 feet.' (No. 19)[39]

The completion of the figure was held up over Christmas because Gaudier had more domestic problems to settle. Sophie was worried about money and by her absence from and control over Gaudier. In addition, interest shown by Mr and Mrs Hare and Macfall had encouraged

Gaudier to look for a new studio; Mrs Hare was particularly anxious that Gaudier should find somewhere more suitable for Sophie in order that she could return to London. The prospects of a new studio were not the only change of fortune. Gaudier signed a new contract in December with Wulfsberg for £10 a month, on a one-year contract, and Lousada made enquiries about purchasing some more sculpture. With these prospects, Gaudier visited Sophie at Dodford for four days at Christmas; they discussed her return to London, but when Gaudier left Dodford they had still not reached any agreement. However, very soon after his return, Mrs Hare found him a studio which he could afford, and he wrote to Sophie to tell her of his good fortune: 'What infinite peace after the hellish din of Redburn Street! Ideas keep rushing to my head in torrents — my mind is filled with a thousand plans for different statues, I'm in the midst of these and have just finished one of them, the wrestler, which I think is very good.'[40]

Gaudier also wrote to Marsh,[41] after some months without contact between them, to tell him that he was moving to his new studio on 4 January at 454a Fulham Road, Studio No. 5, and that he would be pleased to see him there at any time.

From tentative beginnings, 1912 was the year in which Gaudier found a foothold and so made his first sculptural statements. His opportunities, although partly self-created, were also due to the particular help of Macfall and his contacts, the encouragement of Lovat Fraser, and the excitement and stimulation Gaudier obviously felt through Epstein. Frank Harris and Middleton Murry were also helpful, since with Sophie and Brodzky at various times, they provided the other ingredient to success which Gaudier required, namely encouragement.

The year 1912 was therefore a time of expanding ideas, expanding opportunities; and it was only towards the end of the year, as his ideas began to crystallize, that a different characteristic began to emerge in his personality. He began to rely less on others for reassurance and confidence and instead used his friends as buffers for his rapidly increasing self-assurance. During 1913 this characteristic developed, and with it a stronger and more positive style of sculpture. From the letter to Marsh, it can be seen that Gaudier obviously anticipated a better year in 1913. And indeed it was to be a prolific year in his sculptural development, and one of the most significant.

Drawing of Brodzky

NOTES:
1. Letter from Gaudier to Haldane Macfall. 5.1.1912. Victoria and Albert Museum, London. Unpublished. In 1905, Macfall (a biographer and art historian) published two books, *Whistler* and *The Masterfolk*. As a result of his outspoken yet informed opinions, he gathered round him a group of admiring young artists and writers.
2. G. Allfree (1889–1918): painter and draughtsman. Lost at sea on active service. Member of the Haldane Macfall circle. H. C. M. Hardinge: writer and dramatist. Author of *Carnival, Whirlwind* and *A Bowl of Red Roses*.
3. Letter from Gaudier to Haldane Macfall. 15.1.1912. Victoria and Albert Museum, London. Unpublished.
4. Letter from Gaudier to Macfall. 27.1.1912. Victoria and Albert Museum, London. Unpublished.
5. Violet Henson. Letters to the author. June–November 1968. Unpublished.
6. Letter from Gaudier to Macfall. 3.2.1912. Victoria and Albert Museum, London.
7. Letter from Gaudier to Macfall. 12.2.1912. Victoria and Albert Museum, London. Unpublished. Leman Hare trained at the West London School of Art as a wood engraver. He then entered publishing, concerned mainly with art books such as those on the National Gallery and Louvre. An early member of the Macfall circle, where he met Gaudier. Ede, 1, p. 192.
9. Letter from Gaudier to Macfall. 26.2.1912. Part unpublished. Victoria and Albert Museum, London.
10. *The Book of Lovat* by Haldane Macfall. Dent and Sons, 1923, p. 52. C. Lovat Fraser. By 1911 he had established himself in London working as a designer and worked with Gaudier and Gordon Craig on Macfall's *The Splendid Wayfaring*, published in 1913.
11. Diary of Sophie Brzeska. Essex University Library. Unpublished.
12. Letter from Haldane Macfall to Brodzky. 21.11.1919. Victoria and Albert Museum, London. Unpublished.
13. Gaudier's *List of Works*. Kettle's Yard, Cambridge University.
14. Letter from Macfall to Brodzky. 21.10.1919. Brodzky, p. 169. Whereabouts of other works unknown.
15. Letter from Lovat Fraser to Martin Hardie. 4.10.1919. Victoria and Albert Museum, London. Unpublished.
16. Letter from Gaudier to Macfall. 10.5.1912. Victoria and Albert Museum, London. Unpublished.
17. Sketch included in letter from Gaudier to Dr Uhlemayr. 18.6.1912. Private collection. Unpublished.
18. Epstein, *Autobiography*, Hulton Press, 1935.
19. Pound, 1, p. 87.
20. *List of Works.* Kettle's Yard, Cambridge University.
21. Letter from Gaudier to his sister Renée. 19.6.1912. Private collection. Published in part.
22. Letter from Gaudier to Macfall. 1.7.1912. Victoria and Albert Museum, London. Unpublished.
23. *Rhythm* was a magazine started by J. D. Fergusson and M. Murry in 1911, primarily concerned with art, music and literature. It took its title from the excessive use of this word in discussions on the arts.
24. Later smashed by Brodzky, George Banks, Sophie and Gaudier. Brodzky, 1, p. 46.
25. Journal of Katherine Mansfield. Edited by J. M. Murry.
26. Diary of Sophie Brzeska. Essex University Library. Unpublished.
27. Postcard from Gaudier to Sophie. 20.9.1912. Private collection. Unpublished. Also a large number of unpublished letters from Murry to Mansfield and Gaudier. Private collection.
28. *List of Works.* Kettle's Yard, Cambridge University. Work since destroyed in wartime bombing. Letter from A. Lousada to the author. 26.6.68.
29. Letter from Gaudier to Marsh. 25.9.1912. New York Public Library. Unpublished.
30. Letter from Gaudier to Sophie. 24.10.1912. Essex University Library. Part published: Ede, 1, p. 168.
31. Letter from Gaudier to Fraser. 16.12.1912. Mercury Gallery collection, London.
32. Letter from Mr R. Smythies to H. S. Ede. 17.2.1929. Private collection. Unpublished.
33. *Contemporary Portraits.* Frank Harris. Third Series.
34. Letter from Gaudier to Sophie. 25.11.1912. Essex University Library.
35. Epstein, *Autobiography*, Hulton Press, 1955.
36. Letter from Gaudier to Sophie. 28.11.1912. Essex University Library. Ede, 1, p. 209.
37. Letter from Gaudier to Sophie. 30.11.1912. Essex University Library. Ede, 1, p. 215.
38. Letter from Gaudier to Sophie. 3.12.1912. Essex University Library. Ede, 1, p. 216.
39. Letter to S. V. Bacon. Private collection. Unpublished.
40. Ede, 1, p. 224. Whereabouts unknown.
41. Letter from Gaudier to Marsh. 31.12.1912. Victoria and Albert Museum, London.

3

Sculptural development

1912 *to* 1913

The excitement of moving to his new studio was such that Gaudier had to tell someone of his good fortune. Sophie was seemingly unmoved by his enthusiasm in spite of a lack of correspondence between them for nearly six months, so Gaudier wrote two letters, the first to Dr Uhlemayr:

On the advice of some friends and patrons, English 'mecenes' [Maecenases] without generosity, I have taken this studio in the hope that it will bring me more work. Anyhow I can work better here than in ordinary rooms — though what I really want to do is to sculpt a large statue in hard stone, but for that I must first get a commission. All this year I have been reduced to doing little statues in plaster and bronze and portraits which haven't in the least satisfied my desires or my ability. The struggle for life is hard here, worse than elsewhere because all these wretched people are without sensibility, without heart, attracted only by what is eccentric or odiously pretty. To arrive at anything one must either wait for ages or prostitute one's art.[1]

The second letter Gaudier wrote was to Horace Brodzky:

I gathered your address from Rider's shop in St Martin's Court and I should be delighted to make your acquaintance. You will be welcome at my place, address as above, and I would be pleased if you could pay me a call this Wednesday 8th. inst. at about 8. p.m. We'll have some supper together and enjoy conversation.[2]

In addition to this invitation to Brodzky to make a new friend, Gaudier frequently met Edward Marsh during January.[3] Marsh visited Gaudier's new studio with Rupert Brooke,[4] and entertained him with others at Frith Street and gave sympathetic encouragement. Gaudier, unfor-

tunately, was still caught between two restrictive demands, on the one hand his dependence for income on Wulfsberg, on the other his dependence on patrons for commissions for his sculpture. Gaudier's reference in his letter to Uhlemayr expressing his wish to work in hard stone was probably a goal which he had set himself much earlier, in 1912, but with little hope of achievement. This ambition coloured his attitudes to sculpture in 1913 and gave him a purpose.

Towards the end of 1912 he had completed a satirical self-portrait and took it early in January to Lovat Fraser's studio, where he left it on display. Gaudier called the work *Idiot Boy* amongst other titles, and it was the subject of much ridicule between himself and Fraser.[5] This head did, however, bring about a meeting with a young poet and journalist called John Cournos, who, like Gaudier, was struggling to come to terms with both art and literature in London. Russian-born but living in America he had given up his job as an art critic on the *Philadelphia Record* to visit Europe. Cournos saw the portrait in Fraser's studio and as a result of his admiring it, Gaudier invited him to visit his studio.[6] So began another friendship, which, with Brodzky completing the trio, frequented either the Fulham studios or Brodzky's apartment.

Early in 1913 Frank Harris returned from America. Gaudier still regarded him as a possible patron; the portrait bust which had been started earlier was again taken up, and Harris inflated Gaudier's ego with promises of commissions and more work. On the strength of these promises of better prospects Gaudier again tried to persuade Sophie to return to London and in mid-February she conceded. She arrived to find the Fulham studios a dilapidated mess and a solicitor's writ that it should not be used as a residence. The overall effect of the shock of this, the draughts, noise and dirt were too much for Sophie, and within a week of arriving in London she was in bed suffering from the cold, influenza and worry.

Although upset by Sophie's illness and concerned that she did not like the apartment, Gaudier was still optimistic about the future. In February he met another of Haldane Macfall's friends, Sidney Schiff, who, on their first meeting, encouraged him enthusiastically to continue with his sculpture, saying that success was certain. Like Marsh, Sidney Schiff had gathered around him a group of young artists, many of whom, by March 1913, were also included among Gaudier's friends. Amongst these were Curry and his mistress Dolly Henry, Mark Gertler, and probably Stanley Spencer. Throughout March and April there were many evenings spent at the Schiffs' house with a variety of young artists and writers, and in this atmosphere Gaudier thrived, 'arrogantly arguing his opinions and often with little thought for others'. This arena did, however, provide him with the opportunities which he needed to test his ideas, and it was certainly during these months that he consolidated the opinions he had collected from many sources for so long. At the same time he struggled to find ways and means to express them in sculpture.

In March he completed the portrait bust of Harris, but in spite of promises from him and all the other influential people he had met, he was still without a major commission. Part of a letter to Dr Uhlemayr written at the time describes his frustration:

'I am in the midst of a portrait of a writer called Frank Harris and he promises that in a few months everything will be going well with me. It's about time for I am a little discouraged; I have suffered frightfully from all manner of miseries since I left Germany, doing all kinds of jobs and if in the end I can give myself up entirely to my art I shall be the happiest man in London.'[7]

Gaudier's frustration expressed itself in other ways as well; in the destruction of the portrait bust of Murry and the reclaiming of the drawings reproduced in *Rhythm*. What sparked off this attack is not certain, but Gaudier, who had been extremely upset by the whole affair with Murry and Mansfield, met a Scottish artiste 'George' Banks, who had also contributed to the magazine and who had earlier 'wiped the floor' with Murry after a disagreement. Gaudier, encouraged by this and incited by Sophie and Brodzky, went to visit Murry in his rooms together with Miss Banks. Murry recalled the incident vividly:

'I was scared to be alone. In retrospect it seems fantastic, but there is no doubt that at this time — the spring of 1913 — I was really horrified of what Gaudier might do to me.'[8] This incident was followed, perhaps immediately, by a brick-throwing competition between Gaudier, Brodzky and Sophie at the portrait head of Murry. The account by Brodzky[9] relates that after several misses his brick

destroyed the head and so concluded any relationship with Murry. The earlier encounter had terminated the friendship from Murry's point of view also, since he wrote to Katherine: 'G. and Gaudier have just been. Of course I am not worth a twopenny damn now. I've been crying out of sheer nervous reaction. . . . I love you — but suddenly this beast has fouled everything.'[10]

Commemorative of this whole incident is a small relief head on the back of which are inscribed initials which almost certainly refer to Zosik, Murry, Pik and Katherine (No. 20). This episode is important in understanding Gaudier's temperamental nature; once upset he was cruel and vindictive and his sometimes irrational behaviour lost him a number of friends who could have helped him.

Brodzky seems to have enjoyed these encounters and their friendship flourished. Sophie has described the relationship between Gaudier and Brodzky: 'Brodzky was like a dog running in and out of Henri's legs,'[11] while Brodzky has suggested that he was 'really the only friend Henri had.'[12] Their friendship was certainly strong and Gaudier sketched portraits and also started work on a relief carving (No. 21) and a portrait head in clay (No. 22). Brodzky in return was to paint a portrait of Sophie, much against her will. With his pronounced features and lethargic manner, Brodzky was a complete contrast to Gaudier, whose incisive abrupt manner left him unruffled. Brodzky seemed oblivious to the frequently offensive tirade which assailed him from both Gaudier and Sophie and consequently had some kind of attraction for them both.[13]

At about this time Gaudier also met Alfred Wolmark, a painter, who was better established than Gaudier, but

Gaudier working on Seated Woman (*No. 67*)

who was not well known. Wolmark was in touch with the developing attitudes both in London and abroad and both Epstein and Gaudier were particularly encouraged by his authoritative confidence in them. Wolmark provided Gaudier with food and some money, but more important than this he listened and discussed, helping Gaudier to form his own ideas. He was attracted to Gaudier, who, in return for kindness to him offered to model his portrait (No. 23).[14] This portrait, together with one which he modelled of Brodzky at this time, reveal an important change in style: assured, positive, even arrogant.

The friendship with Brodzky progressed, Cournos continued to visit Gaudier's studio, and together with Epstein, whom Cournos also knew, they visited galleries and museums, particularly the British Museum, and occasionally met other friends at the Café Royal. In his autobiography, Cournos described the high-spirited quality of Gaudier's character 'dancing like a young savage down the street singing Carmagnole at the top of his voice and jumping over the pylons at the gate of Hyde Park Corner'. In return for friendship Gaudier was often generous, too generous at times. Cournos also described how he presented him with 'an elaborate statue' and said, 'If ever you are hard up and can sell it, I have no objection.' The subject of the alabaster statue was *Weeping Woman*, and, explaining the reason for the choice of subject, Gaudier told Cournos that the stone was too short for a fully erect figure. 'The size and shape of the alabaster were responsible for making her a sentimental woman weeping.'[15] Another carving which Gaudier started during his friendship with Cournos and Wolmark was *Sepulchral Figure*, carved in Bath stone (No. 25).[16]

Macfall and Hare together with Schiff now managed to persuade him to exhibit his first sculptures, and on 26 June Gaudier triumphantly sent Marsh two tickets for the London Salon Exhibition on the following Friday at the Albert Hall. Although Brodzky attributes the origin of Gaudier's interest in participating in the exhibition to Walter Sickert,[17] he later suggested that it may have been the result of interest by Macfall and particularly Hare, and that 'Epstein also knew about it'.[18] Many artists from abroad were invited to exhibit their work, and Gaudier's excitement at being included was quite justified; he could not have realized how important its consequences were to be.

Six of his works were accepted:

(Cat. No. 1212) L'Oiseau de Feu. *Bronze.*
Loaned from Lousada

(Cat. No. 1213) Wrestler. *Plaster.*
From his Studio

(Cat. No. 1214) Maria Carmi. *Plaster.*
Loaned from Owner.

(Cat. No. 1215) Haldane Macfall. *Plaster.*
Loaned from Owner.

(Cat. No. 1216) Horace Brodzky. *Plaster.*
Loaned from Owner.

(Cat. No. 1217) Alfred Wolmark. *Plaster.*
Loaned from Owner.

Neither the *Wrestler* nor the *Madonna (Maria Carmi)* were sold, but Gaudier and Sophie do not seem to have been disappointed by this, since in the press comments on the exhibition his name was mentioned in the same paragraph as Epstein and Brancusi. Brodzky states[19] that Gaudier met Brancusi when he visited the exhibition. Whether this is true or not he must certainly have been impressed and fascinated by the three children's heads exhibited by Brancusi,[20] one of which was described as 'more like a motor lamp than a human head'.[21] This exhibition brought Gaudier's name before the public. P. G. Konody wrote in the *Observer* on 13 July:

M. Henri Gaudier Brzeska is somewhat difficult to follow in his busts of Brodzky, Wolmark and Haldane Macfall, the first two of which are executed in a kind of frenzied Cubism that is certainly calculated to attract attention, but fails as much in conveying a sense of the sitter's character and appearance as the more normally treated head of Macfall. The artist's failure in portrait is the most surprising as his *Madonna*, a portrait statuette of Maria Carmi in *The Miracle*, provides unmistakable evidence of rare ability.[22]

Ezra Pound visited the exhibition with his friend Osbert Sitwell; they toured the rooms and came upon the *Wrestler*. Pound, making several humorous attempts to pronounce the name of the sculptor, was suddenly confronted by Gaudier, who pronounced the name, saying he was the sculptor. Having quietened Pound's 'impudent manner'[23] he turned on his heel and left. Pound was impressed, perhaps as much by the man as the sculpture, and immediately invited him to dinner.[24] Nina Hamnett, who had heard of Gaudier indirectly, prior to the exhibition at the Albert Hall, also had work exhibited, and on one of her visits there saw a man whom she presumed was Gaudier, looking at her pictures; 'he smiled at her but they did not speak.'[25] Hamnett had obviously wanted Gaudier to introduce himself to her but since he did not she left, determined to meet him.[26]

Gaudier and Brodzky were still meeting Harris and through Harris there still came many promises of wonderful opportunities. Harris said he would buy a carving of a marble dog (No. 26) for £5, and also suggested that Gaudier should go to China with him. The visit to China did not materialize but Harris did purchase the dog. Gaudier meanwhile concentrated even more on his sculpture and spent much of his time during the first weeks of August on an alabaster figure (No. 27), which was a direct development of the *Sepulchral Figure* and was the forerunner of his next important carving,[27] *Singer*

(No. 28). Gaudier must have gained confidence from this carving, but he was still limited by not having enough stone to carve, and by the time *Singer* was complete, he was no nearer to getting any work commissioned. His hopes of success were again raised by his introduction to Paul Morand, secretary to the French ambassador. He was, firstly, infuriated when Morand told him he would show some of his drawings to his father, who was director of 'Arts Décoratifs' in Paris, and he in turn perhaps would get an opinion on them from Maillol or Rodin. But Morand was enthusiastic about Gaudier's work and towards the end of September he returned with the Ranee of Sarawak, who, although she did not commission any sculpture, purchased about a dozen drawings for £10, which at least was some financial encouragement for his efforts.

This money was the first income Gaudier had received for any of his work for about eight months and with it he and Sophie decided to take a holiday at Littlehampton. One reason for the holiday was Sophie's health, which had rapidly deteriorated during her stay in London, partly due to the discomfort of Fulham Road and partly due to her concern over her now rapidly dwindling life savings, on which they were still both dependent. The holiday was no more successful than their life together in London; Gaudier could not wait to get back to London and Sophie was irritable. To relieve the tension, one day they decided to visit Arundel Park; it was one of the happiest days they spent together. They watched the deer and saw a stag

Drawing of the boy Lunn

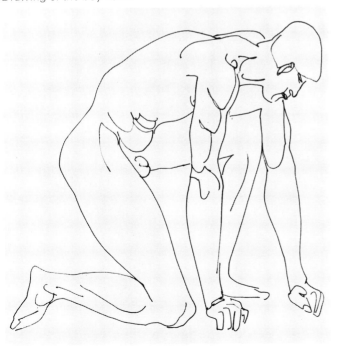

following a group of does. The impression made by this visit was later reflected by many animal drawings and one of Gaudier's most significant sculptures.

Gaudier returned alone to London the day after, and two days later described a return visit to Epstein's studio in a letter to Sophie:

Epstein, he is making some extraordinary statues which are absolute copies of Polynesian carvings, with noses like Brancusi — we stayed there all the afternoon. . . . From there we went to the Café Royal — on the way we met Brodzky. We sat with Epstein, his wife, a French engineer called Norbel and Augustus John who looked as if he would explode. While we were drinking someone called out to me and I turned round to see Marsh with Mark Gertler, I had to talk to him and he invited me to dine with him next week. I accepted. On Monday morning I sorted out my place at Bishop's Road and yesterday morning I went to Putney with Fabrucci.[28]

Important reference in this letter is made to Epstein's 'Brancusi-like noses and copies of Polynesian work', which suggests that Epstein as well as Gaudier had been influenced by Paris and the July exhibition. The fact that Gaudier was obviously discussing Brancusi's work with Epstein adds further weight to the supposition that over the months up to this date Epstein had talked to Gaudier about his enthusiasms for the new movements in Paris as led by Brancusi, Picasso and Modigliani, and elaborated his own interest in the primitive. Gaudier had already made his own observations (Epstein was not speaking to the unconverted), and although Gaudier certainly had no collection, like Epstein, of primitive carving, his knowledge of the ethnographical sections of the British Museum was comprehensive. Even Sophie chided Gaudier for his 'drawings of men with Brancusi-like heads', which accusation he denied, saying 'that they were a direct evolution from his old work and that his sculpture had become quite abstract'.[29] His defence of his own position was quite natural since he had been excited by the primitive long before he met Epstein; the modern movement simply convinced him that his earlier ideas had been correct. But Sophie was not pleased, her reply to his letter was uncompromising and bitter, and at a time when Gaudier was on the verge of finding himself in his work her main worry once again recurs, money. Writing to her in October Gaudier almost dismisses her as a nuisance, an interruption to the real business with which he was now involved:

Rant and rave as much as you like, it has not the slightest effect on me as long as you worry about material things. If you want to stay at Littlehampton I don't want to persuade you to come here, not likely, your little ways are far too gentle at the moment. . . . Since you will tell me to go to the devil I return the endearing compliment with interest.[30]

Their relationship had almost irretrievably broken down. Sophie wanted security, Gaudier now had his sculpture. Fabrucci had a rented studio in a railway arch at Putney, and Gaudier was anxious to have enough space to work. He negotiated with him to rent half this arch,[31] and helped him build a partition to divide it. In order to sell enough work to pay the rent, Gaudier needed to appeal to patrons; he had to sell work to live, since his rejection of Sophie meant he had to be independent.

Fascinated by Gaudier, Nina Hamnett had made further enquiries about him through a London bookseller, Dan Rider. As a result, Rider arranged for them to meet, Nina's excuse being that she knew a lady who wanted lessons in sculpture at 5/– an hour. Having met, Nina invited Gaudier back to her flat, and as they walked up Charing Cross she recalled him asking her:

'What do you do? . . . Yes, of course, I remember it, you are the young girl who sat with my statuettes; my sister and I called you "La Fillette".' We walked on. He gave my friend lessons, and one day came to my rooms and said, 'I am poor and want to do a torso, will you sit for me.' I said 'I don't know, perhaps I look awful with nothing on,' and he said 'Don't worry.' I went one day to his studio in the Fulham Road and took off all my clothes. I turned round slowly and he did drawings of me. When he had finished he said 'Now it is your turn to work.' He took off all his clothes, took a large piece of paper and made me draw, and I had to. I did three drawings and he said, 'Now we will have some tea!'[32]

Almost certainly as a result of this relationship with Hamnett, Gaudier produced three successive pieces (Nos 29, 31, 32) which do not fit into the pattern of his abstract development as a sculptor. Gaudier's own comments about the sculptures must be regarded as his real feelings. Undoubtedly these three works show an ability not previously revealed in his sculpture, and yet his own dismissal of them as 'hollow' shows that he was seriously concerned to find an original means of expression and was not satisfied to adopt any acceptable style. Since he had little regard for them, none of these works was exhibited at the Grosvenor Gallery; instead Gaudier sent a crouching male figure.[33] The sculpture was broken and before submitting it Gaudier had gilded over the damage. Surprisingly, the work was sold, but since he had not paid his hanging fee an argument broke out with the gallery, Gaudier finally walking out in a fit of temper without payment.

In spite of his lack of money Gaudier was still included in dinners and discussions. Marsh still entertained groups of young painters, and it was through these meetings that Gaudier continued to meet many new artists. In July Gaudier had introduced Marsh to Mark Gertler[34] and in succeeding months, whenever Gaudier was entertained by Marsh at Raymond Buildings, Gertler was always the centre of attraction. His other new friend, Ezra Pound, also showed particular kindness to him. Pound knew Epstein, and during late October, November and December Pound not only 'discovered' the potential of both men but helped them to clarify their own thinking by his analytical and sensitive understanding of their problems. Pound, of course, was also a founder member of groups such as the Iagistes, and gradually drew both Gaudier and Epstein towards contact with this group and most importantly, later, with Wyndham Lewis and T. E. Hulme.

Sculpting was now the most significant part of Gaudier's life. The problem of acquiring stone was partly overcome by obtaining it from a stonemason's yard late at night with Nina Hamnett keeping watch for the police, or from the offcuts of sculpture being worked by Fabrucci.[35] *Mermaid* (No. 33), a most sensitive carving, is likely to have been carved from such an offcut. A description of Gaudier's studio at this time was recorded by Nina Hamnett:

Drawing of a woman, 1913

In the next arch of Putney Bridge there lived an academic sculptor who did monuments. He did not carve stone, so Henri despised him; he had a band of Italian workmen who came and did the dirty work for him, that is to say they hacked out the stone. When the sculptor was out Henri would buy the workmen some Chianti and learn from them how to carve stone. He bought a forge cheaply and put it in his backyard. There he used to forge tools[36, 37] that he sculpted with. It was a wonderful machine with large bellows and made a great noise. Henri said to me, 'Don't mind what people say to you, find out what you have in yourself and do your best, that is the only hope in life.'[35]

In late September Hamnett also introduced him to Roger Fry who had started the Omega workshops,[38] a workshop for the design and manufacture of modern art and furniture. Fry had said he would like to meet Gaudier and could perhaps give him some work. In November, in addition to getting access to materials at the Omega workshops, which in itself was worth a great deal to him, Gaudier also sold the *Dancer* to Sidney Schiff for £10. The price paid by Schiff included the making of a round pedestal for the figure,[39] and when on 1 December he received the second part of his payment, the first having been made on 14 November, he wrote to Schiff:

I am naturally glad that Mme Schiff likes the statuette. It is a sincere expression of a certain disposition of my mind, but you must know that it is by no means the simplest nor the last. The consistency of me lies in the design and the quality of surface — whereas the treatment of the planes tends to overshadow it.[40]

In addition to this work, a visit by Raymond Drey to the Putney studio in November resulted in a commission for a marble carving for £5. The subject of the carving was the clay figure of a sleeping fawn which he saw in the studio (No. 40). Drey particularly remembered Gaudier arriving at his London hotel some weeks later, dishevelled and dirty, carrying the carving in an old sack inside his coat.

Gaudier's continued employment at the Omega workshops allowed him the opportunity to explore other materials. He carved *Maternity* (No. 34), created a number of designs for trays (No. 36), modelled a cat (No. 37), from which a number of casts were glazed and fired, and also carved a statue of a boy (No. 38) in alabaster. It is hardly surprising that when we study Gaudier's treatment of animals in sculpture many of the works produced are small and sensitive, seemingly created in order to reinforce his understanding of animal forms. These provided a base for his search for a greater inner understanding of the problems of simplification of form, line and mass with which he struggled in his major works.

During 1913 Gaudier had gradually become acquainted with many young avant-garde painters and writers in London and although there were no formal meetings, varying groups were often to be seen at the Cabaret or the Tour Eiffel Restaurant. Lewis, Pound and Epstein all knew each other, and it was not surprising therefore to find that, when Lewis drew round him a 'determined band of anti-futurists', Gaudier was amongst them. He was on the fringe of the group, but on 20 November Marinetti and Nevinson were due to lecture at the Dore Gallery on Futurism, and Lewis had assembled his group of about ten friends, including Gaudier, at Greek Street, where after a good meal they, 'shuffled bellicosely round to the Doré Gallery. . . . Marinetti had entrenched himself upon a high lecture platform. Gaudier went into action at once. He was very good at the parlez-vous, in fact he was a Frenchman. He was swiping about him without intermission standing up in his place in the audience all the while. . . . The Italian intruder was routed.'[41] Gaudier was from that moment at the centre of the group, committed, determined. His primitive, arrogant confidence naturally appealed to Lewis, under whose guidance his sometimes previously thwarted need for expression found new opportunity. Almost overnight, therefore, Gaudier projected himself as the leader of the group.

Lack of correspondence from Gaudier, together with a letter informing her that he had found a friend in Nina Hamnett, made Sophie so worried and jealous that she returned to London without warning. But Gaudier was so engrossed in his activities that she was a positive nuisance to him. She complained, as usual, about lack of money and about the rooms at Bishop's Road. To such criticism Gaudier replied:

I despise people who complain, if I am earning nothing at the moment, that doesn't matter at all, it is sure to come. Everyone is his own master, and the weak naturally perish because they haven't the strength to fight. . . . I am an artist and nothing but art has any interest for me. So long as I do good sculpture, I don't care how I arrive at it.[42]

His last sculpture of 1913 was probably *The Embracers* (No. 41). This carving achieved a new dimension for Gaudier, but it also left a number of unsolved problems relating particularly to the three-dimensional quality of his carving and the relationship of each facet of a carving to the complete work, problems which were partly resolved in the other sculpture of this period, *Crouching Figure* (No. 35). One factor which emerges strongly by the end of 1913 is how Gaudier had come to terms with his materials. The earlier rough-hewn heads were forgotten together with the deliberations and searchings of earlier years, and a new style of work emerged in some of his sculptures. Significantly amongst these were the torsos, which gave him confidence and assurance, and allowed him to move freely towards areas of abstraction in his continued search for a personal style of sculpture. The rate of Gaudier's sculptural development was only achieved as a result of complete dedication of purpose, and it is evident from his letters, drawings and sculpture during 1913 that he readily assimilated many new ideas. One must also consider how far he was able to differentiate between those ideas, and during 1914 it is interesting to see how the influences of Pound, Lewis and Hulme, Rodin and primitive sculpture were juxtaposed in his struggle to find himself.

The apparent arrogance and conceit with which Gaudier conducted his social life during 1913 continued the pattern of 1912: anyone who was likely to deter him from his own objective was abruptly pushed aside. 'So long as I do good sculpture I don't care how I arrive at it.' It was with the same determined attitude that Gaudier faced the year 1914.

NOTES:
1. Letter from Gaudier to Dr Uhlemayr. 6.1.1913. Kettle's Yard, Cambridge University.
2. Letter from Gaudier to Horace Brodzky. 6.1.1913. Collection L'Instituit Néerlandais, Paris. Published incorrectly in Brodzky, 1, p. 13 as 6.1.1912. Horace Brodzky was born of Jewish parents in Melbourne, Australia in 1885. He was educated in America and then earned his living as an illustrator, before coming to London early in the 1900s.
3. Gaudier's letters to E. Marsh. Jan. 9, 3, 21, 1913. New York Public Library. Previously unpublished.
4. C. Hassell, *E. Marsh, A biography*, p. 207.
5. H. Brodzky. Interview with the author. 1968.
6. J. Cournos, *Autobiography*, Putnams N.Y., 1935.
7. Letter from Gaudier to Dr Uhlemayr. 12.3.1913. Kettle's Yard, Cambridge University.
8. M. Murry, *Between Two Worlds*. Published 1935. G . . . refers to Georges Banks. (Should not be confused with Gaudier–Pound references to 'M'lle "G"'.)
9. Brodzky, 1, p. 48.
10. Interview with author 1968.
11. Sophie's diary. Essex University Library.
12. Interview. Brodzky with the author. 1968.
13. Brodzky, 1, p. 67. Details of sitting. Also interview with the author. 1968.
14. Interview. F. Wolmark with the author, 1969.
15. J. Cournos, *Autobiography*, Putnams N.Y., 1935.
16. *List of Works*. Kettle's Yard, Cambridge University.
17. Brodzky, 1, p. 67.
18. Brodzky. Interview with the author. 1968.
19. Brodzky, 1, p. 94.
20. The three heads were: *Child's Head*, bronze. *Child's Head*, marble. *Child's Head*. Ref. Jianou, p. 79.
21. *Illustrated London News*. 12 July 1913.
22. *Observer*. 13 July 1913.
23. Sophie's diary. Extract recounting these incidents. Essex University Library.
24. Pound, 1, p. 46. Denied by Sophie writing in her copy of Pound, 1. Private collection. Kettle's Yard, Cambridge University. 1969.
25. Sophie's diary. Essex University Library.
26. Sophie's diary. Extract described Nina Hamnett as a 'dilettante really only interested in seducing young artists'. Essex University Library.
27. Sophie's diary. Essex University Library.
28. Aristide Fabrucci was a little-known Italian stonemason and sculptor who established himself in London between 1880 and 1885.
29. Ede, 1, p. 235. Reference unknown.
30. Letter to Sophie. 10.10.1913. Essex University Library.
31. Rent returns signed by Fabrucci 1913–14. Private collection.
32. N. Hamnett, *Laughing Torso*.
33. Grosvenor Gallery: 'International Society of Sculptors, Painters and Gravers'. Autumn Exhibition No. 8, *The Golden Figure*. Gilt plaster. Untraced.
34. C. Hassel, *Edward Marsh*, p. 232.
35. Nina Hamnett, *Laughing Torso*.
36. Brodzky. Interview with the author. 1968.
37. These tools were spindles provided for him by Mr Raymond Drey. Interview with Mr Drey by the author. 1968.
38. Sophie's diary. Essex University Library. The Omega workshops were announced by Roger Fry in *Art Chronicle* on 26 April 1913. It represented 'a new movement in decorative art. . . . It will embrace the making of "character" furniture which will reflect the artistic feeling of the age.'
39. Since destroyed.
40. Letters from Gaudier to Sidney Schiff. Selected parts: November 14, December 1, 1913. Unpublished.
41. Wyndham Lewis, *The Artist*, pp. 144, 145.
42. Sophie's diary. Essex University Library.

4

Towards
sculptural
maturity

1913 *to* 1914

By the beginning of 1914 Gaudier had established a number of friendships within various groups in London. There were those close friends of 1913, Nina Hamnett and Horace Brodzky, and the developing relationship with Ezra Pound. The introduction to the Omega workshops, in 1913, had enabled Gaudier to meet many artists previously unknown to him, and, in spite of the division of the workshop over the Ideal Home Exhibition,[1] Gaudier managed to continue his work there for several months and maintain a friendship with Fry, Wyndham Lewis, Wadsworth, Hamilton and Etchells. By January 1914, however, he was quite clearly more sympathetic to Lewis and his followers than to Fry, and it was probably only because materials were available at the workshop studios that he continued to frequent them.

Marsh and Macfall were, of course, less significant at this time, but Gaudier continued to see Marsh irregularly if only in the hope that he would buy some sculpture.

All Gaudier's sculptures were now directed towards one major objective, simplification of form. His drawings reflect his thinking closely, and the combination and interdependence of drawing and sculpture emerges more strongly at this time than at any other. The plaster relief of *The Wrestlers* (No. 42) illustrates this well. But perhaps the work which best exemplifies it is *Red Stone Dancer* (No. 43), which was completed early in 1914.[2] The importance of the work is its uncompromising simplification and directness. The earliest dancer, posed for by Hamnett, was a compromise; this work, which was a development from it, is not. *Red Stone Dancer* is more abstract than anything Gaudier had previously produced, and is a sculptural statement of Gaudier's use of pure form. It is in this sculpture that the influences of Lewis and of Hulme are seen to be interpreted in the positive extension of

earlier experiments in the simplification of form. The triangle and circle are here 'asserted'. The figure is 'designed with spiralling thrust of positive movement'.

As can be seen in comparison with *The Wrestlers*, the treatment of the hands is similar, but whereas in that work they become a termination of a line and a form, in this sculpture they follow the direction of the forces within the figure and accentuate them. The triangle used on the head is repeated in shapes within the legs and arms, and the circle of the breast, directly beneath the head, is more strongly emphasized to add further weight to the extended arm of the figure. Pound's comment on this sculpture is particularly perceptive:

This last almost a thesis of his ideas upon the use of pure form. We have the triangle and circle asserted, *labled* [sic] almost, upon the face and right breast. Into these so-called 'abstractions' life flows, the circle moves and elongates into the oval, it increases and takes volume in the sphere, or hemisphere of the breast. The triangle moves toward organism, it becomes a spherical triangle (the central life-form common to both Brzeska and Lewis). These two developed motifs work as themes in a fugue. We have the whole series of spherical triangles, as in the arm over the head, all combining and culminating in the great sweep of the back of the shoulders, as fine as any surface in all sculptures. The 'abstract' or mathematical bareness of the triangle and circle are fully incarnate, made flesh, full of vitality and energy. The whole form-series ends, passes into stasis with the circular base or platform.[3]

Many of these qualities are also present in another work which must be closely related to this time: *Maternity* (No. 44). The mother figure in this carving is closely associated with *Red Stone Dancer*, and it is really the different quality in the two stones which exaggerates their differences. Whilst working on these sculptures Gaudier maintained his contact with the Omega workshops. Certainly he was anxious to find opportunities for displaying his work before the public, and the fact that Fry organized the Alpine Club exhibition in January 1914 may have been reason enough for him to remain in contact. Certainly some of the work exhibited was only as a result of Fry's influence, and it seems from the catalogue that Gaudier was 'allowed' to exhibit *Red Stone Dancer* in return for the four other works: *Vase* — marble, *Boy* — alabaster, *Fawn* — stone, *Cat* — marble; from which Fry obviously hoped to make some money. We know from Gaudier's *List of Works*[4] that Fry required a quarter of the cost on commission for these sculptures, and since Gaudier produced several fawns at about this time, it seems likely that he regarded most of these sculptures as fodder in return for getting larger and better quality stone for the 'real' sculptures like *Red Stone Dancer*.

Gaudier in front of Hieratic Head of Ezra Pound, *1913–14*

Gaudier's sculptural development is littered with distractions, which he was obliged to complete from financial necessity. One example of this was a casket carved for Pound and his friends for a presentation to W. S. Blunt, a poet and writer. The main reason for the presentation was described by Pound in *Poetry*, March 1914, as 'in token of homage', and this respect can only be attributed to the admiration held by Pound and his friends for Blunt's vehement opposition to the British Empire and its institutions. Eight poets, including Aldington, Flint, Manning and Yeats, presented Blunt with this token of their respect for him, as represented in the small casket carved by Gaudier (No. 49).[5] As a sculpture it is insignificant, yet it illustrates the confusion caused by a sculptor, who, in the same month that he had completed *Red Stone Dancer*, could also carve such a piece of work. This inconsistency has previously been attributed to a lack of real understanding, and it is from such inconsistencies that Gaudier has been termed a follower rather than an innovator.

January and February were busy months, for although he had no commissions to work on he had the combined encouragement and support of Pound, whose friendship with him at this time was at its closest. Pound provided a large block of stone, out of which Gaudier was to carve Pound's portrait head. There was a great deal of discussion between them as to the form of the portrait head, and the many sketches which exist today illustrate how their thinking helped to simplify on paper the basic design for the stone. The final form of the head was termed 'phallic' by some, 'hieratic' by others. There is certainly within its final form the concepts of a bold, arrogant simplification which by this time Gaudier had adopted as his most expressive style. To dismiss this work as a joke[6] is to presume that once again Gaudier was only concerned to appease his friend Pound. But this carving was produced at a time of real artistic activity, and was the best and largest block of marble Gaudier had ever carved to date. There are many similarities, notably in its arrogance, to the Wolmark and Brodzky busts, and the freedom which Gaudier had felt months earlier when tackling these was obviously experienced again in this work.

This was not the only encouragement for Gaudier. Pound, using all his influence, persuaded the *Egoist* magazine to reproduce photographs of his work as visual support for an article discussing 'The New Sculpture'.[7] This article reviewed the content of a lecture given by T. E. Hulme to the Quest Society on 'Cubism and New Art at Large'.[8] T. E. Hulme had, of course, been lecturing in London during 1913 on subjects such as the philosophy of Bergson, but in this lecture he championed, amongst others, Epstein. Hulme's position was clearly anti-Futurist, he supported Lewis's art with theoretical argument and not unnaturally Gaudier felt sympathy towards him also. Gaudier's own philosophical comprehension was far less than Hulme's, but earlier in 1911 and in 1912 he had grappled with the ideas of Bergson himself. His own style of work had searched for vital terms of expression and, just at the point when his work was beginning to achieve that elusive quality, he found in Hulme an exponent of logic whose philosophical ideas were founded in his own understanding. They were each attracted to the other.[9] Gaudier's exuberance was at its highest, and, in spite of the fact that he sold nothing from the 'London Group' exhibition at the Goupil Gallery, his long struggle to come to terms with his own ideas at last seemed worthwhile.

'So long as I have tools and stone to cut, nothing can worry me, nothing can make me miserable. I have never felt happier than at this moment.'[10] Not only was he happy, but confident, arrogantly confident, and together with Pound's encouragement they set something of a trap in the *Egoist* which 'Auceps' [the author of an article in a previous issue of the *Egoist*] rose to, and provided Gaudier with his first opportunity in print. Pound explains in his book on Gaudier that he had set up the situation in an earlier article in the *Egoist* by writing: "Let us confess that we have derived more pleasure from the works of Wyndham Lewis than from the works of Poussin and Apelles." We had bet that Auceps would reply to this by pointing out that the works of Apelles no longer survived the wear of time, and Auceps gratified us by doing so in the next number of the *Egoist*.'[11] Gaudier's reply contained a scholastic attack interspersed with emotional responses. 'It would be better if he had the courage to say, "I am a dry intellect and I can understand but to feel is impossible." The modern man is a sculptor who works with instinct as his inspiring force.' Many of these phrases echo statements in earlier letters to Sophie.

March was a busy month; the portrait head for Pound was hard work and took up a great deal of time. The cutting of the marble was considerably slowed down because Gaudier had poor tools, and anyone who happened to be near the studio would be called upon to help him operate Fabrucci's portable forge while he tempered his chisels.[12] Apart from the piece from which the head was carved Gaudier still had little or no other stone on which to work. Consequently, he continued to visit the Omega workshops where he had free access to materials, and the availability of this facility allowed him to continue to explore ideas, one of which was another interpretation of the earlier marble vase (No. 54).[13] From small offcuts of stone, many toys or playthings were carved during the following months.[14] These carvings cannot be considered as major landmarks in his development but do illustrate how the maturation of his style by 1914 had in fact produced a consistent sculptural concept. Typical works of this emerging style are *Duck* (No. 55) and *Dog* (No. 56) carved from marble, both of which show how even in his more relaxed moments his thinking continued in abstract terms.

Gaudier still maintained his contact with Marsh. Early in the month he had dined with him at the Chantecleer, together with Stanley Spencer,[15] and later the same month he was at the Raymond Buildings, again with another group of artists. During the next few months Gaudier was drawn quite frequently to the group of artists which met at Raymond Buildings in the evenings to discuss many aspects of art.

The month of March was also particularly important, since prior to that date the 'Omega Rebels' had continued to meet at the workshops. Now Lewis, with the help of Kate Lechmere,[16] rented 38 Great Ormond Street, which was then named the 'Rebel Art Centre'. There were no official meetings of the group; Lewis painted there on Saturdays, and Wadsworth, Roberts, Etchells and Bomberg were all frequent visitors in the early months. Hulme was in constant contact with Lewis and the others as well, and was also attracted to Kate Lechmere. As a result also of his friendship with Epstein, he occasionally brought him within the spirit of the group although neither was an actual member. Perhaps it was understandable that neither joined since Lewis jealously guarded Kate Lechmere, and Gaudier by his earlier utterances had identified himself, and was accepted, as the sculptor of the group. Although as a group they had now rejected Omega, each had depended on it as individuals, and for Gaudier its usefulness continued, if only to provide him with commissions and sometimes materials.

Work on the Pound head continued and by early April it was complete. Gaudier's pride in the finished work was quite evident. Encouraged by Pound, photographs had been taken of the head while it was being carved, and, if only as a physical feat, he had mastered the block of stone and 'won it' (No. 50).[17]

Regular meetings of different sections of the 'Omega Rebels' were taking place throughout April and Pound and Lewis came closer together in their united attack against mediocrity. Pound often visited the centre on Saturdays when Lewis was painting, and Lewis allowed him to see his recent work, which was kept locked in a back room to prevent imitation.[18] The strength and support which Lewis gained from Pound was similar to that which Gaudier had received, and so it was not surprising that the three of them were, by mid-April, well involved in the planning of the first issue of *Blast*; in fact its advent was announced on the back of the *Egoist* of 15 April in an advertisement entitled 'End of a Christian Era'.

In addition to these associations, the meetings with Marsh continued; Gaudier was generally the only sculptor present at evenings where the painters Spencer, Gertler and Curry, Curry's mistress, Dolly Henry, and others discussed modern art. Gaudier benefited less than the others from Marsh's patronage, since he was too proud to let him know his real poverty and frequently talked in a manner which understated his really desperate financial position.[19] It is not certain which sculpture can be definitely dated to this time, but it seems likely that a number of works were produced in addition to *Duck* and *Dog* out of small offcuts of stone. There is one other sculpture which is definitely related very closely to the quality and shape of the original material, namely *Imp* (No. 57). As a result of his studies in the ethnographical sections of the British Museum Gaudier had become fascinated not only by the forms of the figures but also by the subjects holding bowls and supporting platforms. He had made drawings of carvings done by the Afo and Baluba tribes, and consequently he produced an experimental group of figures which were directly influenced by these studies (No. 59).

In May the Pound bust was exhibited at the White-chapel Gallery in an exhibition of twentieth-century Art. Unfortunately it was not supported by *Imp* or other recent work, but by a variety of apparently unrelated works, some of which Gaudier possibly thought would attract a buyer. The only reason he was able to afford to transport such a large carving was that the gallery paid the costs,[20] and so Pound's hieratic head was exhibited for the first time. Other sculptures included were *Figure, Maternity, Firebird, Cat* and *Fawn*.[21] The lack of success in selling work from this exhibition made absolutely no difference to Gaudier; it was almost as if he expected not to sell his work and no longer regarded such a sale as recognition of success. In 1913 he had exhibited six works by invitation in the Allied Artists' exhibition, and in May 1914, as a result of successful canvassing (by Gilman and Gore in particular), he was elected chairman of the artists' committee.[22] Work was also in progress on another stone carving, this time a commission which had come to him through Fry and the Omega workshops. Brodzky explained[23] how two huge blocks of stone were delivered outside the Putney studio for him to carve into two large garden vases. The blocks of stone were enormous, the task almost impossible, his chisels broke and the roughing out of the work started very slowly. The maquettes for these sculptures are however of interest, as they have origins in *Maternity* (No. 44), the *Vase* statuette carved in marble, and the two-figure model of *Men with Bowl*. They are also unmistakably derivative from African tribal sculpture, although in their development the figures have gained some resemblance to the upstretching infant in *Maternity*. The two maquettes for the vases were created in plaster, but the second is far less interesting since it is a development and abstraction from the upper portion of the supporting figures. The models survive but the sculptures in stone were never completed.

Gaudier now became interested in metal, in particular brass. A number of records describe how small offcuts of metal became small extensions of his larger work. These toys delighted friends such as Pound, Hulme and Lewis, and Kate Lechmere recalled how Lewis had 'several of Henri's toys in his pockets'.[24] This new interest in metal

may be attributed to Hulme, and it is the strongest link which can be established between them both. Modern art was under the critical examination of Hulme's uncompromising scrutiny. He wrote:

In the new art there is a desire to avoid those lines and surfaces which look pleasing and organic, and to use lines which are clean, clear-cut and mechanical. You will find artists expressing admiration for engineers' drawings, where the lines are clear, the curves all geometrical . . . you will find a sculptor disliking the pleasing kind of patina that comes in time on an old bronze and expressing admiration for the hard clean surface of a piston rod.[25]

With Hulme not only expounding a process but dictating its terms it is not surprising that Gaudier was torn between different interpretations of sculptural ideas. He was experimenting in basic forms derived from primitive sculpture and at the same time working with geometrical ideas in metal. *Charm* (No. 58) and *Door-knocker* (No. 62) are good examples of these latter experiments, which he faced with almost childlike enthusiasm. Also *Brass Toy* (No. 63a), although probably made as a toy for Hulme, was also in essence a real expression of Hulme's ideas on sculpture, as is also the case with *Fish* (No. 64). Gaudier claimed to cut these forms directly from brass, as he also cut *Knuckle-duster* (No. 65a & b) for Hulme. Kate Lechmere's recollection about these shapes was that they were a less serious side to Gaudier's work, a comment also supported by Brodzky's comments:

He would tell me so and so wanted a watch-chain, a door-knocker, or a paper-weight — something 'phallic', to use their words. About this time the word 'phallic' was very popular and commonly used as a part of the art jargon of the day. Brzeska would cut a piece of brass for them that would look more like a masonic charm than anything else. He would tell them that it was symbolic of fecundity or vitality, or whatever exotic nonsense he had in his head at the time.[26]

The explanation given by Kate Lechmere of the knuckle-duster, once owned by Hulme, concurs with this account. In his book Pound also discusses Gaudier's and Hulme's interest in metal.[27] 'These experiments in small abstract form interest me. It interests me that Mr Hulme in his boyhood should have pestered the village blacksmith week in and week out to forge him a piece of metal absolutely square.'

If Gaudier had simply interpreted Hulme's philosophical ideas in three-dimensional forms, he certainly also assimilated Hulme's thinking, particularly in his drawing, which now explored the projections of these ideas. The question must therefore again be asked as to whether Gaudier was purely 'performing to order', or whether the substance underlying Hulme's ideas had any real value for him. June 1914 certainly showed that he had not only absorbed the thinking but developed through it. *Bird Swallowing a Fish* (No. 66) is the sculptural statement which confirms this development.

Gaudier had become so absorbed with his sculpture that he often even slept in his studio under the railway arch, and Sophie led an almost separate existence. By early June, however, the summer heat brought an infestation of bugs to the apartment, which Sophie could not tolerate, and she again left Gaudier and London for Littlehampton. Their relationship had been less strained over the first six months of 1914, partly because Gaudier had ignored many of her demands, and they had gone their separate ways. One unfortunate aspect of her departure was that it left Gaudier with no money at all and he had to write to Sophie to ask for some almost as soon as she had gone. 'Send me ten shillings . . . since you left I have only three pounds, and most of that I have had to spend on things for my work, so for the last four days my

Drawing of man and horse, 1914

cat and I have lived on milk and eggs given me on credit, and it isn't enough; my stomach is already dreadfully upset, and I haven't a halfpenny.'[28] Fortunately Sophie sent him some money.

June was also the month for the summer exhibition for the Allied Artists' Association and as chairman for the year, Gaudier was called upon to write a criticism of the exhibition.[29] This is Gaudier's longest published article and he obviously used it to express a number of his most committed ideas. Also in the same publication is a letter to the editor in which Aldington, Bomberg, Etchells, Wadsworth, Pound, Atkinson, Hamilton, Roberts and Lewis, together with Gaudier, signed a group statement disassociating themselves from Marinetti and Nevison and the *Futurist Manifesto* published in the *Observer* on 7 June. The English Vorticists were asserting themselves.

However, a sense of concern and anticipation hung over France and England with the assassination of Franz Ferdinand of Austria on 26 June, and Gaudier reacted to this more sensitively than one would have expected. There were a number of sculptures in the process of development in his studio: he was involved in aspects of a theme centred around bird and fish forms and was also working on a seated female figure. On 9 July, ominously, he wrote out the *List of Works*, a copy of which was printed by H. S. Ede in 1931. This action alone is inconsistent with his usual carefree manner and may have been prompted both by the fear of war and Sophie's return to London with new ideas as to how they could make more money and attain a better standard of living. There is no doubt that Gaudier would have been aware of how serious international affairs had become, since he was still in contact with Marsh. Early in July[30] he and Brook had dined with Marsh, later going on to the ballet at Drury Lane, where they had met Lady Ottoline Morrell. Although it is unlikely that the centre of conversation would have been politics, the possibility of war cannot have escaped mention.

The other important occurrence of the summer months was, of course, the publication of *Blast*, which had been advertised, 'to be issued in June'. The publication was celebrated by a dinner, itself postponed a week to 15 June, at the Dieudonne Restaurant in Ryder Street. The outburst over the publication temporarily distracted many people from the subject of possible war. It was in fact a war in its own right and 'blasted' everything. Gaudier's contribution was no less outspoken; in fact it was an expertly prepared outburst, which, within the magenta covers, carried equal importance with writings by Lewis and Pound. The writing of such a précis could only have been done by a man who was as committed and as confident as Gaudier. Pound called it a 'synthesis';[31] and it is indeed a synthesis of everything Gaudier had learnt, emphasizing the salient points not only of the history of sculpture but of the formulation of its prin-

Drawing of horse's head, 1914

ciples.[32] This statement is a complete précis of everything that had preceded it, and even including Gaudier's reflections on his struggle 'to survive in the complex city'.

It is therefore interesting to examine what work Gaudier was producing whilst planning this article and what was produced in the following weeks. Although Pound dates *Seated Woman* (No. 67) as the last major work of 1914, there is evidence to suggest that this sculpture was probably completed by late June 1914 and was not his last major work.

Recalling Gaudier's comments on the *Bird* in the summer exhibition, it is significant that his last major sculpture was therefore another carving which was based on this subject, *Birds Erect* (No. 68).

Although Brodzky dismissed this carving as a 'two-dimensional design', it has within it the expression of understanding related to organic and natural growth formation previously more tentatively searched for in works such as *Stags* (No. 52). Although abstract, and concerned with many of the earlier problems of the inter-relationship of surfaces, planes and masses, this carving expresses an inner feeling of structure, growth and strength. The forms are interdependent yet individually poised and the contoured surfaces and divisions of the stone give the carving a natural beauty. For Gaudier this work was a positive development from *Bird*.

With the growing concern of war, an air of depression hung over Gaudier. Nina Hamnett recalled how depressed he was, and how they walked together in Richmond Park and Gaudier talked about the threat of war and his resolve to return to France.[33] On 20 July Marsh visited the Putney studios[34] but bought nothing; Gaudier gave him a few drawings which he had admired, no doubt in return for Marsh's kindnesses to him. Macfall also wrote to him, care of the Rebel Art Centre, and Gaudier coldly replied that he was welcome to call on him at any time, but offered no suggestions of a date or time.[35] With the threat to his homeland, sculpture was dismissed, and his vow never to return to France was forgotten.

On 4 July war was declared; on 5 July Gaudier wrote what can only be described as his will, signed H. Gaudier over a one-penny stamp with Ezra Pound's and Dorothy Shakespeare's signatures.[36] It took very little time for him to decide where his duty lay, and he left England for France. In the last sculptures which Gaudier completed before his departure it can be seen that he was nearer to achieving his objective of a personal means of expression than at any time during the previous three years.

The year 1914 was, in fact, a progressive development towards a realization of this style, but it is quite evident that although Gaudier could clearly define the purpose and aims of his sculptures, he was still struggling with the problems of the inter-relationship of forms, and the direction of planes within these forms. Although in *Birds Erect* and *Seated Woman* he had avoided the 'hard edge geometric' pressures of Hulme, this problem was most likely to occur again in future sculptures.

It is true to say that Gaudier's sculpture still lacked a characteristic style, but certain subjects such as birds and animals, and particular human poses with the arm raised over the head, had by this time become repeated vehicles of expression for him. It also seems likely that the clarity of thinking demanded by writing articles and criticisms, particularly under the scrutiny of Pound and Lewis, helped him to crystallize his own ideas. It could also be argued to the contrary that they compelled him to find a means of expression suited only to their needs. It is only possible to support or reject this argument, on the basis of the statements which Gaudier himself made about his work several months after he had left England for France.

NOTES:
1. Roger Fry to Wyndham Lewis. 10.10.1913. Ref. *Apollo*, March 1970.
2. Sophie's diary. Essex University Library.
3. Pound, 2, 1957, pp. 137–8.
4. *List of Works*. Kettle's Yard, Cambridge University.
5. Meeting at Newbuildings Place, 18 January 1914.
6. Brodzky, 1, p. 58.
7. *Egoist*, 16.2.1914. Drawing *Boy with Rabbit*. Photograph. *Singer* and *Sepulchral Figure*.
8. Quest Society Lecture, 22 January 1914, 'Modern Art and its Philosophy'.
9. Interview. K. Lechmere with author. 1968.
10. Sophie's diary. Essex University Library.
11. *Egoist*, 16.3.1914, and Pound, 1, p. 33.
12. Raymond Drey. Interview with author. 1969.
13. Raymond Drey. Interview with author. 1969.
14. Brodzky. Interview with author. 1968.
15. Postcard. Gaudier to Marsh. 5 March 1914. Victoria and Albert Museum collection. Unpublished.
16. Interview. Kate Lechmere with author. 1968–9.
17. Interview. Kate Lechmere with author. 1968–9. Also Sophie's diary. Essex University Library.
18. Interview. Kate Lechmere with author. 1968–9.
19. Brodzky. Interview with author. 1968.
20. Interview with H. Brodzky. 1968.
21. Brodzky, 1, p. 176. This is the only record of which sculptures were exhibited.
22. Letter. Frank Rutter to H. Brodzky. 22.9.1933. Copy taken at interview with author, 1968. Unpublished.
23. Interview. H. Brodzky. 1968.
24. Interview. Kate Lechmere with author. 1968–9.
25. T. E. Hulme. *Speculations*, p. 97.
26. Brodzky, 1, p. 90.
27. Pound, 1, p. 167.
28. Ede, 1, p. 261. Not dated. Whereabouts of this letter unknown.
29. The *Egoist*. 15 June 1914 (Reproduced).
30. Letters of Sophie Brzeska. Essex University Library. Refers to this meeting with Marsh, 'Henri had come home very depressed'. Marsh was Private Secretary to Winston Churchill from 1905–1922.
31. Pound, 1, p. 25.
32. *Blast*. July 1914. *Gaudier Brzeska Vortex* reproduced.
33. Kate Lechmere. Memories of discussions with Nina Hamnett 1915. Interview with author 1968. See also Nina Hamnett autobiography.
34. C. Hassell, *E. Marsh*, p. 289.
35. Letters. Gaudier to H. Macfall. London, Victoria and Albert Museum. Unpublished.
36. Will. Private collection. Unpublished.

Sophie Brzeska

5

THE STRUGGLE TO SURVIVE

1914 *to* 1915

Drawing of machine-gunner, sent from the trenches, 1915

The remainder of Gaudier's life was primarily that of a soldier. We have already seen that when he was faced with a specific problem he devoted his entire enthusiasm and interest to it. This was also true of his life as a soldier. Not surprisingly his involvement in art and sculpture sometimes took second place to the struggle to survive in the trenches, but his interest and enthusiasm for art could not be suppressed, even by war.

In the same way as his output of sculpture had been prolific in the previous eighteen months, now his writing was prolific, and during the next nine months he wrote at least eighty letters. These letters are the complete and only record of this period and in them he curiously re-established contact with all the friends he had ever made, and with his family, whilst his relationship with Sophie faded. Under the pressure of war, Gaudier reveals a truer quality of character, in that he is worried by death and war and delighted by the beauties of nature. The war therefore polarized his real beliefs and by its ghastly destruction Gaudier was compelled to face both his past and the future.

In an article written from the trenches these points are clearly defined.

'Life is the same strength

It would be folly to seek artistic emotions amid these little works of ours.

This war is a great remedy. In the individual it kills arrogance, self-esteem, pride.'

Gaudier also wrote several times to his parents and this can only be interpreted as his statement of appeasement for earlier transgressions. In fact his parents responded with full affection and concern, and it must have been reassuring for him, in the early horrors of war, to receive their support and forgiveness. In commentaries on Gaudier's life little is made of the consequences of his parents' affection, but this must have confirmed his resolve and convinced him that in his defence of his homeland he had not only redeemed the past but rightly fulfilled his duty.

With the novelty of war growing tedious the context and attitudes in his letters change, and in October art and sculpture are mentioned for the first time. Jokingly he suggested to Pound, 'I do not despair of ever reaching Düsseldorf and bringing back the finest Cézannes and Henri Rousseaus to be found up there.'[1] He also promised to send him an essay on sculpture for the Christmas number of *Blast* and added, 'Please let them reproduce in it a photo of your bust. I shall send the essay as soon as finished, but all depends upon the fighting. If we have a few quiet days you'll have it soon.'[2]

The months of October and November were quite mild apart from occasional frosts at night, and although conditions in the trenches were not good, Gaudier had not experienced the horrors of knee-deep mud and severe cold. Consequently November was a productive month and the article for *Blast* was completed.[3, 4]

During this period he also wrote to Mrs Bevan telling her, 'I have carved a *Maternity* out of the butt of a German rifle. The Captain has it.'[5, 6] It has also been said that Mrs Bevan received a small carving from Gaudier at the Front and since there is no mention in any correspondence to her about when she received it, it seems most likely that, if it was carved at the Front, it was carved in these months before the severity of the winter set in.

Gaudier mentioned the rifle-butt in a letter to Pound but not the toothbrush handle carving (No. 69).[7] However, since the unusual nature of the material, smoked bone, distinguishes this sculpture from other carvings it is notable that a smoked-bone carving appears in Gaudier's *List of Works* written before he left for France. The entry details give the owner of the work as Madame Karlowska, Mrs Bevan, 14 Adamson Road, Hampstead, and describe the carving as 'Ornament: taille dans manche de brosse à dent et enfume. Poli.' Although the evidence is not conclusive it suggests that earlier datings of this sculpture (as the last carving) may not be correct.

As a soldier Gaudier was daring and determined and, although death brings about rapid promotion in war, his progress through the ranks was quickened by his ability. Although Sophie stated[8] that Gaudier was promoted on 1 January it was not until he wrote to Mrs Bevan on 9 January and Wadsworth on 8 January that he told anyone of his promotion. In a letter to Wadsworth he wrote, 'News! I have been promoted to the high rank of corporal for service in the field.'[9] But winter in the trenches was really appalling, and every letter during these last two months was filled with comments on the horrors and discomforts of war.

We have had to stand in ditches with a foot of fluid mud at the bottom for four days at a time . . . there are 800 Germans dead on the ground behind the trench which we cannot bury.[10] When we took the trenches, it was a sight worthy of Dante . . . the close vicinity of 800 putrefying German corpses . . . I got a sore throat in this damned place.[11]

Not surprisingly sculpture was not mentioned again until February and then in a letter to Wadsworth he discussed what sculpture or drawings he had done which might be suitable for exhibition and said he might even send a

Drawing of an exploding shell, sent from the Front, 1915

drawing from the trenches.[12] Within four days he had despatched 'the two less worst drawings I have done since I have been in the trenches',[13] and written to Pound telling him the price he wanted for the sale of his work. 'There is a big marble, a sleeping woman[14] which you have never seen . . . for the present I am quiet, still and happy . . . but I have some presentiment it is the great calm preceding violent storms, for which we are now well prepared.'[15]

Gaudier wrote more frequently to Kitty Smith, in one letter enclosing a photograph of himself, 'Perhaps you will recognize me in the back row of the group I send you; the sun was strong and I could not look straight.'[16] A second photograph he sent to his parents and this remains the last photographic record of Gaudier at the Front; it is obviously later than the photograph sent to Kitty Smith and was probably sent to his parents in the middle of May.[17]

In two letters to Mrs Pound he gives one kind of description of life in the trenches, which contrasts with descriptions he had written to other friends.

I am just now quartered in trenches (in the middle of them), they are covered with Lily of the Valley, it grows and flowers on the trench itself. In the night we have many nightingales to keep us company.[18]

Today is magnificent, a fresh wind, clear sun and larks singing cheerfully. The shells do not disturb the songsters. In the Champagne woods the nightingales took no notice of the fight either. They solemnly proclaim man's foolery and sacrilege of nature. I respect their disdain.[19]

This latter statement reveals yet again an aspect of Gaudier's character which had been continually put aside in his struggle to survive, and the fact that it recurs at this point only adds further evidence to the argument that

Photograph taken at the Front. Gaudier is fourth from left, 1915

when the opportunity occurred he returned to a natural relationship with plants and animals. Earlier, for Christmas, he had sent Mrs Bevan sycamore seeds, and in this letter of 20 May to Mrs Pound he wrote, 'I become rather interrupted because of the enemy . . . I tell you they'll end up by wounding me. All I can give you from here is a buttercup, the only flower that grows on the trench (we are in meadows) and not a very nice flower, but it is a souvenir from the fights at the Neuville.'[20]

Noticeably there is an absence of correspondence with Sophie and little is known to exist, although Gaudier may have written frequently to her. Sophie's diary[21] gives the only insight into this period but the diary was written after Gaudier's death, and contains statements expressed in great anxiety and mental disturbance. Some comments, however, do complete an understanding of their relationship at this time.

You left for the war — tearing my heart in pieces. We did not indulge in much affection, I, because I was thrown out by your departure, and also by your conduct during much of the previous year. I thought you did not really love me any more, a little yes, and that truly from the depths of your heart, but my candour and the fear I had of realizing an ugly truth held me a little on my guard. You did not write to me nearly so often as I wanted and all that gave me great cause for apprehension.[22]

The relationship with Sophie had become far less important once Gaudier was removed from her direct influence, and although parts of Sophie's diary suggest that their relationship was re-established, Gaudier was preoccupied with other friends, war and survival. Writing to Pound in early June he described his feelings:

I have written to Mrs Shakespeare in what a nice place I was. It becomes worse and worse. It is the tenth day we are on the first line. . . . It is a gruesome place, all strewn with dead, and there's not a day without half a dozen fellows in the company crossing the Styx. We are betting on our mutual chances. Hope all this nasty nightmare will soon come to an end. What are you writing? Is there anything important or even interesting going on in the world? I mean the 'artistic London'. I read all the 'poetries' in one of the *Egoists* Mrs Shakespeare sent along. Away from this and some stories of Guy de Maupassant and E. Rod, I have read nothing, a desert in the head is a very inviting place for a Boche bullet or a shell, but still it had better not choose this place, and will be received in the calf for instance.[23]

'In a single attack by the First and Seventh on the village of Neuville St Vaast, houses D^3 to D^{12} were captured, taking over also the left of the main street, and the houses bordering it. This result was achieved by 3.30 p.m. on 5 June 1915. The ninety-five men killed in the action included the Sergeants Rocher, Buisou, Gaudier . . .'.[24]

Photograph of Gaudier with fellow soldiers, kneeling on the left at the back, 1915

NOTES:
1. Letter from Gaudier to Pound. 11.10.1914. Pound, 1, p. 60.
2. Letter from Gaudier to Pound. 24.10.1914. Pound, 1, p. 64.
3. Letter from Gaudier to Pound. 9.11.1914. Pound, 1, p. 62.
4. *Blast*. Reproduced.
5. Letter to Mrs Bevan. 12.11.1914. Private collection. Unpublished.
6. Letter from Gaudier to Wadsworth. 14.2.1915. Private collection. Unpublished.
7. Letter from Gaudier to Pound. 1.12.1914. Pound, 1, p. 63.
8. Sophie's diary. Essex University Library.
9. Letter from Gaudier to Wadsworth. 8.1.1915. Private collection. Unpublished.
10. Letter from Gaudier to Wadsworth. 16.12.1914. Private collection. Unpublished.
11. Letter from Gaudier to Pound. 18.12.1914. Pound, 1, p. 63.
12. Letters from Gaudier to Wadsworth. 14.2.1914. Private collection. Unpublished.
13. Letter from Gaudier to Wadsworth. 18.2.1915. Private collection. Unpublished.
14. This probably refers to *Seated Woman*.
15. Letter from Gaudier to Pound. 20.3.1915. Pound, 1, p. 68.
16. Letter from Gaudier to Kitty Smith. 6.4.1915. Private collection. Unpublished.
17. Photograph from 'Un Artiste de Chez nous insoumis et patroite'. Original owned by Mme Baillet Gaudier. Copy given to the author 1969.
18. Letter from Gaudier to Mrs Pound. 14.5.1915. Pound, 1, p. 76.
19. Letter from Gaudier to Mrs Pound. 19.5.1915. Pound, 1, p. 78.
20. Letter from Gaudier to Mrs Pound. 29.5.1915. Pound, 1, p. 78.
21. Sophie's diary. Essex University Library.
22. Extracted translations from part of the diary of Sophie Brzeska. Essex University Library. Unpublished.
23. Letter from Gaudier to Pound. 3.6.1915. Pound, 1, p. 69.
24. Translated from the official report as used for B.B.C. Broadcast. R.P. Number 1097.

Conclusion

Ezra Pound expressed his own personal loss on Gaudier's death by writing: 'His death at Neuville St Vaast is, to my mind, the greatest individual loss which the Arts have sustained during the war.'

It is of course worthless to surmise what Henri Gaudier might have achieved had he not been killed at Neuville St Vaast. Yet what had he achieved by the age of twenty-three, an age when many artists have done very little?

In the early years of the century, as an indirect consequence of the break-up of the New English Art Club and the reaction against Impressionism, there emerged in London various small groups of artists and intellectuals. Gaudier's arrival amongst them was fortunate; it allowed him to learn of their extremes and associate himself with those ideas which he understood or admired.

The artistic atmosphere in London was conducive to learning and from an 'immature foreigner', he rapidly developed to become a sculptor of repute. The reputation he gained was as a result of a number of highly individual sculptures, and, although in themselves they were original pieces, it cannot be said that Gaudier ever achieved a recognizable style.

The richness of London's museums and art galleries was particularly important to Gaudier; being self-taught, his learning was all from first-hand experience and he was dependent on these original sources for ideas and inspiration. Few self-taught artists had made such use of this kind of research and it is evident from the way Gaudier organized his learning that one of his most outstanding talents was that he digested these influences with ease; and, more importantly, he used them to produce original ideas. This facility, and his acquisitive nature, are important factors in his sculptural development. The term 'eclectic' has often been used derisively in relation to Gaudier, but because of his versatile mind and above-average intelligence he was able to learn quickly, and consequently his so-called 'eclectic' artistic achievements were in fact a direct result of his understanding.

'Regarding my visit to the British Museum, I took particular notice of all the primitive statues, negro, yellow, red and white races, Gothic and Greek, and I am pleased to say that I am now certain of one thing which had bothered me for a long time, whether the conventional forms in primitive sculpture, which give enormous satisfaction through serene happiness or excessive sorrow, and are produced by positive movement synthesized and directed only towards one end, do not reveal an understanding more at one with nature, in other words greater and with more understanding, than the modern sculpture of Pisani, Donatello and up to Rodin and the French today. . . . Having carefully thought about these comparisons, at present, I think not, but how far I am correct I cannot say. . . . All this means that I feel I am an individual, a Pik Gaudier Brzeska and it is my individual feeling that counts the most.'

From the days of his early childhood, as recorded by his father, up to the last letters enclosing flower petals sent from the trenches, Gaudier was at one with nature. His love of animals, birds and plants became so much a part of his artistic expression that it can easily be overlooked. The animal drawings he produced began in childhood with studies of insects and were later followed by animal studies in the Bristol and London zoos, the stags in Richmond Park, and included innumerable sketches of other animals, even his studio cat. These drawings convey an intimate understanding of animal life, with unique sensitivity. Similarly, in his animal sculptures and bird forms, particularly in the small toys he carved for Pound and Hulme from odd pieces of green stone, one feels that he makes real and personal statements. In addition to these small sculptures, larger works like *Stags* still retain something of the same intimate affection, and it may be that in these sculptures and drawings we can see Gaudier working most naturally and successfully. Gaudier's comments on animal life are unique.

Gaudier's response to and love of animals is not unrelated to another of his particular achievements, his 'coming to terms' with the tools and materials of the sculptor. Having decided not to paint, but to concentrate on sculptural forms, Gaudier had his own difficulties, particularly in his lack of basic knowledge of the materials and processes of stone carving. Accepting that some of his early stone carvings reveal this inadequacy, his later work shows not only a sympathy for stone but what can only be described as an innate response to it. He did, of course, receive particular help from Epstein in the early stages of his carving, but Epstein's role as an avant-garde sculptor was sometimes uncommitted, and consequently Gaudier was a lone pioneer in establishing new values within this process. As a result, he not only helped to revitalize what had come to be recognized as merely a craft process, but he gave to it both subject-matter and terms of expression which were to re-emerge fifteen years later. And it was in the carving *Maternity* that Gaudier achieved one of his most accomplished sculptures. This work must be seen as a significant achievement, which was later to be used as a starting point for other sculptors such as Henry Moore.

In dismissing Epstein as an 'uncommitted leader', it must also be remembered that he did in fact perform another very important function. He was one of the main sculptural links between Paris and London, and at a time when Gaudier was searching for direction to his ideas, Epstein's informed opinions about attitudes in Paris spurred him to continue his own enquiries. Epstein was one of the few English artists who had first-hand knowledge of the Paul Guillaume collection of African sculpture, and to Gaudier, who had been studying primitive art in the British Museum, this was exciting news. Surprisingly, therefore, Gaudier was not remote from the developing ideas of other sculptors; indeed, Epstein's accounts of Picasso, Brancusi and Modigliani only gave him more encouragement and a greater determination.

But although Gaudier knew of the Cubist developments in Paris, there is no evidence to suggest that he was acquainted with the experimental developments of Cubism, such as those made by the Duchamp brothers at the Puteaux studios. As we have seen, Gaudier's own experiments and discussions of Cubist ideals had led him to be as involved as the Puteaux artists in discussing all matters of current interest which could have any influence on sculpture and art in general. There can be no doubt that the meetings held at the houses of Schiff, Hare, Macfall and Marsh acted as an intellectual catalyst for him, and in consequence many of his sculptural explorations were partly developed in theoretical terms on these occasions.

It seems most likely therefore that, through his own particular study of primitive sculpture, Gaudier began a gradual process of formal geometric reductions in his sculpture, firstly in experiments in portrait heads in early 1913. Later, in 1914, he developed these in complete animal and human figures. Gaudier of course wrote that he would present his emotions 'by the arrangement of my surfaces, lines and planes', but it is evident when we examine his later work more closely that there are specific examples where he has not only been concerned with these principles, but has reshaped and accentuated the underlying structural framework of the sculpture in order to achieve a new sculptural expression. This is particularly true of *Stags* and *Birds Erect*. And this is not all, for in addition to these concepts, in *Red Stone Dancer*, he adds the dimension of rhythm. Here are Cubust principles in sculptural terms.

Gaudier, unlike Picasso, was not concerned to invent but to translate, and consequently was involved in an individual development of the early geometric solids of Cubism, rather than the later developments of Analytical Cubism. It is also possible to see how he further developed his explorations within these concepts when we examine *Birds Erect*, which was concerned to compose closely related, rounded geometric forms in a rhythmic arrangement of planes. This sculpture, his last major work before his departure to France, must also be regarded as one of his most significant contributions to the development of modern sculpture, and is the more important when considered against his theoretical ideas as expressed in *Blast*.

> 'Sculptural energy is the mountain
> Sculptural feeling is the appreciation of masses in relation.
> Sculptural ability is the defining of these masses by planes.'

If it can be accepted that *Stags* achieved a significant progression for English sculpture, then this statement published in *Blast* has become an equally important tenet. Gaudier expressed in these statements an inner artistic perception of a primary energy and power within nature, which was a motivating force in itself. It was not until 1922 that an English sculptor, Henry Moore, read this statement and appreciated its real significance, and consequently the development and establishment of an English sculptural tradition was assured.

Henri Gaudier must stand at the threshold of what is termed 'the emergence of British sculpture', and in time his contribution to sculpture will be seen to have even wider implications. He was before his time, and achieved a rare, if not unique maturity in his sculpture, unequalled in a man so young. That his sculpture was for so long unrecognized in France and ignored in England is perhaps best explained by Pound when he wrote, 'So terrified are we of a man with an unusual faculty, of a man "burning to speak".'

CATALOGUE
of works

All the dimensions are given in inches,
height first.

1. PORTRAIT OF MY FATHER

1910. Orléans, Musée des Beaux Arts. Dry clay painted bronze. No casts. $10\frac{3}{4} \times 8\frac{5}{8} \times 9\frac{1}{2}$ in.

This bust is Gaudier's earliest known sculpture, it was probably modelled when he returned to St-Jean de Braye in 1910. Gaudier described the bust as 'style natural caractère très exagéré'.

Also illustrated here is a small clay plaque dated 1908 of Minerva, imitating Roman art and reminiscent of a number of drawings done by Gaudier at this time.

2. PORTRAIT MASK OF SOPHIE BRZESKA

*About 1911. Cambridge University, Kettle's Yard. Fired clay. No casts. 10×8 in.
Exhibited: Cardiff 1953 (No. 8, Mask, terracotta £25. 0. 0.).*

This clay portrait mask is badly worn and was lost until 1969, when the author traced its
whereabouts and it was transferred to Kettle's Yard. The mask is referred to in Gaudier's
letters to Sophie and appears in his *List of Works*: 'terre seche, grandeur nature,
proprietaise Gaudier Brzeska conserve souvenir.'

3
MARIA CARMI

1912. Cambridge University, Kettle's Yard. Painted plaster. Nine bronze casts. 21 ×13½ in. Exhibited: London, Leicester Gallery 'Memorial exhibition 1918 (No. 25, plaster); London, Bumpus exhibition 1931 (No. 31, plaster).

This sculpture was commissioned by Mr Leman Hare, who had met Gaudier Brzeska through his contact with Haldane Macfall, a friend of Major Smythies. Writing to Macfall about preparations for the sculpture, Gaudier Brzeska wrote, 'Mr Hare wanted me to make a statuette of Maria Carmi as the Madonna at Olympia — off we went towards 8.00 p.m., tired as could be, made about sixty sketches of the subject. . . .'

The clay model was completed on the weekend of 26 February, and cast into plaster and painted. Gaudier Brzeska was particularly enthusiastic about this first commission since he had a promise through Mrs Hare for selling a cast of it for £50.

The construction of the figure is very basic and reflects in its serene complacency a compromise to Mrs Leman Hare, who was particularly concerned that the work should be colourful and decorative: 'she suggested that I should indicate on the plaster the different colours gold, red and blue, and this I will do.' A number of drawings for the sculpture exist, including a pastel which is very similar to the finished sculpture.

There were originally two plaster casts, the first appears in Gaudier's *List of Works*: 'Sold to Leman Hare, £5. 0. 0.' The second was sold at the Memorial exhibition in 1918.

4. ORNAMENTAL MASK

1912. Geneva, Petit Palais. Painted plaster. Seven bronze casts. 30 ×27 in. Exhibited: London, Memorial exhibition 1918 (No. 45, lent by Baroness d'Erlanger).

This plaster relief, together with other masks and tiles, was originally created for Lovat Fraser. The original plaster was painted in crude, bright colours and gilded on parts of the face. Referring to his experiments at the time, Gaudier wrote: 'Just as simple and bright as can be, I use the optic mixing of the colours — putting them in pure pigments side by side.' The modelling of the mask was obviously based on his study of the primitive carvings and masks in the British Museum, where he was spending a great deal of his time drawing. The sculpture has little relationship, except for the surface decoration, with other work of the period, but was part of an overall search for a sculptural style.

The sculpture appears in Gaudier's *List of Works*: 'Sold to Lovat Fraser, £5. 0. 0.'

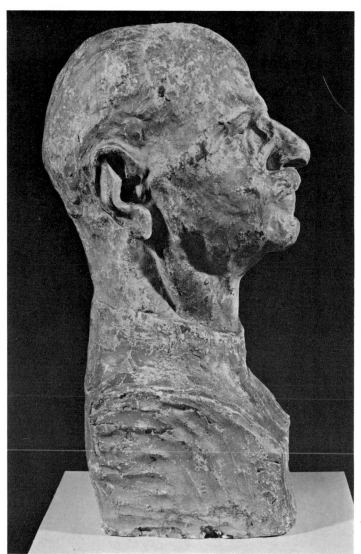 

5. PORTRAIT OF MAJOR SMYTHIES

1912. London, Tate Gallery. Plaster. Six casts in bronze. 43 ×7 ×20 in. Exhibited: London, Memorial exhibition 1918 (No. 97, original plaster).

Major Smythies's bust was the second of two portraits completed by Gaudier early in 1912. The whereabouts of the first is unknown. It was of Haldane Macfall, and it was he who introduced Major Smythies to Gaudier and suggested the portrait bust. At this time Gaudier was very interested in the work of Rodin and, emulating Rodin, didn't require his sitters to sit, and indeed liked them to walk about. Sophie, however, noted that it was a great relief to him when they sat down. Major Smythies was quite delighted with the finished head and paid to have it cast in bronze. In a reply to Major Smythies of 24 April 1912, Gaudier wrote, 'I have retouched the head so that the little that had been spoilt by the wet cloth has come back again. . . . I have asked them (the foundry) for a light green and blue patina of old Pompeian bronze, which, I believe, is what you prefer.' This bronze, a unique cast made for Major Smythies, was given to Manchester City Art Gallery through the N.A.C.F. on 31 March 1922, and remained unique until 1972.

The sculpture appears in Gaudier's own *List of Works*: 'Sold to Major Smythies for the cost of casting: bronze £12. 0. 0. plaster £1. 10. 0.'

6. PORTRAIT OF HALDANE MACFALL

1912. Whereabouts not known. Plaster. No casts known. About 43 ×7 ×20 in. Exhibited: London Salon 1913 (No. 1215); London, Memorial exhibition 1918 (No. 64).

Reflecting Rodin's style of portraits, the head is strongly modelled, particularly in the jaw, mouth and lower nose, and the whole head is a purposeful appraisal of the subject. In the completed work one feels there are attitudes very reminiscent of Rodin's bust of Clemenceau.

The resultant differences between this portrait and the one of Major Smythies could be interpreted as the differing degrees of respect that Gaudier had for his sitters: respect for Macfall, disdain for Smythies; but these two heads were important in his development, since they brought out a practical realization of the sculptor's problems.

Rodin: *Clémenceau.*

7.
HEAD OF A CHILD

1912. Cardiff, National Museum of Wales. Sandstone. No casts. 4 ×3 in. Exhibited: London, Memorial exhibition 1918 (No. 15); Leeds 1943 (No. 72); Cardiff 1953 (No. 11).

This sculpture is the least well known of a number of early stone carvings cut by Gaudier towards the end of 1912. Common to all is the fact that they were only partly cut from the original block of rough stone, and are as crude as his other early attempts at modelling and casting. One of the two heads referred to appears in Pound's book as *'Head of Christ*, a very early work since destroyed by the sculptor'. Pound also refers to a head which he calls *Infant Hercules in Grey Stone*, which he says was broken in moving to the Putney studio. This second head may be the same one which now exists in the collection of Kettle's Yard, carved in sandstone and having the same rough character as the sculpture in Pound's book. As works in their own right these carvings are really only important in showing the beginnings of a transfer from modelling portrait heads to carving them. There are in addition to these two heads a number of other carvings, which, because of their similarity, omission from the *List of Works* and obvious exploratory style, must be included in this period and were probably produced between Gaudier's first meeting with Epstein and early November. These previously undated sculptures follow as Nos 11 and 12.

PORTRAIT OF MISS BORNE

1912. Location unknown. Plaster.
Twelve bronze casts. $16\frac{1}{2} \times 9\frac{3}{4}$ in.
Exhibited: London, Memorial
Exhibition 1918 (No. 101, plaster);
Leeds 1943 (No. 79, bronze); London,
Folio Society 1964 (No. 3, bronze).

This portrait has previously been
known as *Mademoiselle B.* In 1971
the author found that the sitter was a
Miss Borne. Similar in style to the
portrait bust of Enid Bagnold, it is
another example of the early portrait
heads modelled by Gaudier of his
friends in London. Each of the busts
he had previously completed were
searching for a style and a freedom of
expression within the subject, and
although they do not achieve this
entirely they are solid exercises for the
more expressive portraits which were
to follow.

9
HEAD OF A YOUNG MAN

1912. Germany, Stadt Bielefeld.
Sandstone. Twelve casts in artificial
stone. 12 × 9½in. Exhibited:
London, Memorial exhibition
1918 (No. 43, stone 1912); London,
Bumpus exhibition 1931 (No. 36,
Head, stone); Leeds 1943 (No. 70);
Orléans 1956 (No. 9, Tête de Garçon);
London, Arts Council 1956 (No. 6);
London, Marlborough Gallery 1965
(No. 93); Stadt Bielefeld 1969 (No.
8).

This carving and No. 9 seem most
likely to be sculptures carved during
the early months of Gaudier's
friendship with Epstein. At last
Gaudier had found someone who not
only held similar attitudes to his own
but was developing those ideas in his
sculpture. Epstein was to be admired,
almost revered, and certainly for a
period after their first meeting Gaudier
aspired to be a real sculptor in stone
like Epstein. Although no record exists
of stone carvings at this time, there are
two documented attempts at carving
heads in stone which seem most likely
to be of this period.

10. LOVE SCENE

1912. Doncaster, Metropolitan Museum. Seravezza marble. No casts known. $9\frac{1}{4} \times 16$ in. Exhibited: London, Memorial exhibition 1918 (probably No. 60 Nude Man and Woman).

This sculpture, which was lost between 1930 and 1977, is a very good example of Gaudier's growing understanding of the translation of the human figure into two- and three-dimensional form. Whilst the sculpture closely resembles the stylistic qualities of some of the figure drawings of the period, the activity of carving has here developed in him an awareness of line, interrelationship of form and figurative abstraction. The female figure closely resembles the solidity and strength which was to be repeated in later works. The sculpture appears in Gaudier's *List of Works* as 'Scene d'Amour relief. Marble Seravezza 10 × 8 in.'

11. WOMAN

1912. Hull, University Art Collection. Bath stone (Bas relief). No casts known.
22¼×16 in. Exhibited: London, Memorial exhibition 1918 (No. 99).

Like the carvings of stone heads, this sculpture was also one of Gaudier Brzeska's early attempts at cutting stone. The handling of the stone is rough, almost crude, and the arrangement of the relief design is relatively simple, with a variety of depth of contour. There is a monumental treatment of parts of the figure, showing a simplification of design, particularly in the treatment of the breasts, head and arms, while parts of the abdomen and legs seem unresolved.

12. MAN AND WOMAN

1912. Leeds, City Art Gallery. Alabaster, gilded and painted (Relief). No casts known.
8×13 in. Exhibited: London, Memorial exhibition 1918 (No. 38); Leeds 1943 (No. 61).

The bevelled border of this relief carving was originally painted bronze, the remainder of the background was coloured red and the figures yellow. It continued therefore some of the thinking adopted by Gaudier Brzeska for the sculptures *Ornamental Mask* and *Maria Carmi*; but, although he later gilded an alabaster carving to hide a crack in it, this work was the last stone carving to be painted. Stone carvings after this date reveal a concern for the surface quality of the stone, a truth to the material. There are many aspects of this carving which are similar to the relief carving *Woman* (No. 11). The unusual treatment of the face of the woman is a new development in Gaudier Brzeska's experiments, and it is these small details and the more obvious simplification of the arm and thigh which occur in late sculptures as stylistic qualities.

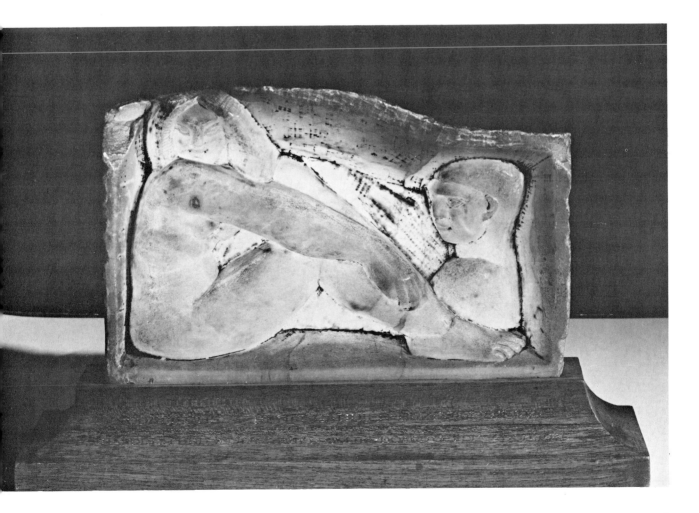

13
MONKEYS

1912. Cambridge University, Kettle's Yard. Sandstone. Twelve casts in artificial stone. 7 ×6¼ in. Exhibited: Cardiff 1953 (No. 13); London, Marlborough Gallery (No. 98); Stadt Bielefeld 1969 (No. 8).

This sculpture does not appear in Gaudier's *List of Works* and was given its title by H. S. Ede. There are several descriptions of sculptures in the diaries and notebooks of both Gaudier and Sophie which could be applied to this work but do not suggest a title for it. It seems more than likely that it was started in 1912 and was added to and altered in 1914, when the triangular designs were cut into the heads of the figures.

14
FIREBIRD

1912. Private collection. Clay (destroyed). Ten bronze casts; three plaster casts (one extant) from original clay model. 24 in. high. Exhibited: London, Allied Artists' exhibition 1913 (No. 1212); London, Whitechapel '20th Century Art' 1914 (No. 179); London, Memorial exhibition 1918 (No. 31); Leeds 1943 (No. 62); London, Arts Council 1956 (No. 2).

This sculpture, a portrait of Adolph Bolm and Tamara Karsavina in the Russian ballet's production of *The Firebird*, was Gaudier Brzeska's second commission, and made for Mr Julian Lousada. Like *Maria Carmi*, executed for Mrs Leman Hare, this work bears little sculptural relationship with the works which preceded and followed it. The sculpture exemplifies Gaudier's search for a sculptural style and compromise to the wishes of patrons, but does, however, also continue a search for a simplification of forms and direction of line, and this process is the essence of later developments in his work. This is the first sculpture in which the artist was concerned with defining sculptural spaces, and the difficulties of the problem are accentuated by the interrelationship of the dancers. The imbalance of the male dancer, being almost counterbalanced by the upward thrust of the female figure, does not achieve a graceful agility but is rather a poised stance. Lousada paid to have one plaster cast in bronze and the other was painted and exhibited in Dan Rider's shop in London, and later sold to Leman Hare for £6. 0. 0.

15. WOMEN CARRYING SACKS

1912. Private collection. Plaster. Six casts in bronze. 13¾×11 in. Exhibited: Orléans 1956 (No. 11); London, Arts Council 1956 (No. 16).

In a letter to Sophie Brzeska in October 1912, Gaudier wrote, 'I am continually modifying my ideas, and I'm very glad to do so. If I stuck to one particular idea, I should grow mannered and so spoil the whole of my development. As far as I can see at this moment, I believe that art is the interpretation of emotions and consequently of the idea.' This sculpture is yet another example of the artist's search for a suitable means of expression, and all the work in clay produced at this time has a similar 'loose' appearance; the clay appears soft and malleable and consequently gives the work a particular flowing quality.

16. GORILLA

1912. London, D'Offay Gallery. Plaster. Eleven bronze casts. 15 ×20 in. Exhibited: London, Memorial exhibition 1918 (No. 33); Leeds 1943 (No. 58).

In return for his assistance in decorating his studio, and as a token of the friendship between them, Lovat Fraser gave Gaudier Brzeska a book of entry passes to the London Zoo. As a result, numerous pen and crayon studies were produced of animals and birds, which in turn provided the stimulus for such sculptures as *Gorilla*. This vigorous interpretation is the more interesting because of the treatment of the arms and chest of the animal, the composition and surface of the modelling, as in *Women Carrying Sacks*, becoming more important than accurate representation. The overall impression of the work is one of strength and assurance, qualities which were soon to be repeated in portrait heads early in 1913.

17
WORKMAN FALLEN FROM A SCAFFOLD

1912. London, Victoria and Albert Museum. Clay (destroyed). Two bronze casts; two plaster casts (one destroyed). $11\frac{1}{2} \times 15$ in. Exhibited: London, Memorial exhibition 1918 (No. 16, plaster); Leeds 1943 (No. 57, clay); Cardiff 1953 (No. 3, plaster); Orléans 1956 (No. 7, plaster).

Although this figure is believed to be a fragment of a figure which lost its arms during the sculptor's lifetime, it shows, perhaps more than any other of Gaudier's works, the influence of Rodin. From letters written during 1912, we know that Gaudier had read Rodin's *L'Art*, and this sculpture seems directly derivative from sculptures by Rodin such as *The Broken Lily* and *The Daughter of Icarus*.

The sculpture continues to demonstrate Gaudier's expressive handling of clay referred to in Nos 15 and 16.

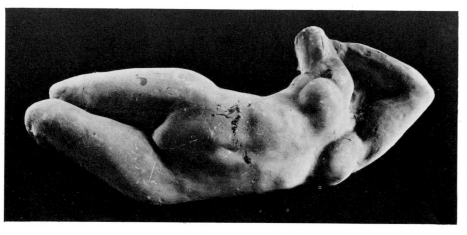

Left
Rodin: *Torso of Adèle*. 1882. Paris, Musée Rodin.

18
HEAD OF AN IDIOT

*1912. London, Victoria and Albert
Museum. Plaster. Seven bronze casts.
6¾ × 5¼ in. Exhibited: London, Memorial
exhibition 1918 (No. 21, plaster).*

This work is considered to be a
satirical self-portrait and as such
displays an element of humour, while
at the same time exploring further
aspects of the simplification of form
which are partly evident in other
portrait busts of 1912. It has also
sometimes been referred to as *Head of
a Jew*, and was exhibited under that
title during the artist's lifetime in the
London bookshop of Dan Rider (see
also No. 14), and also in Lovat
Fraser's studio.

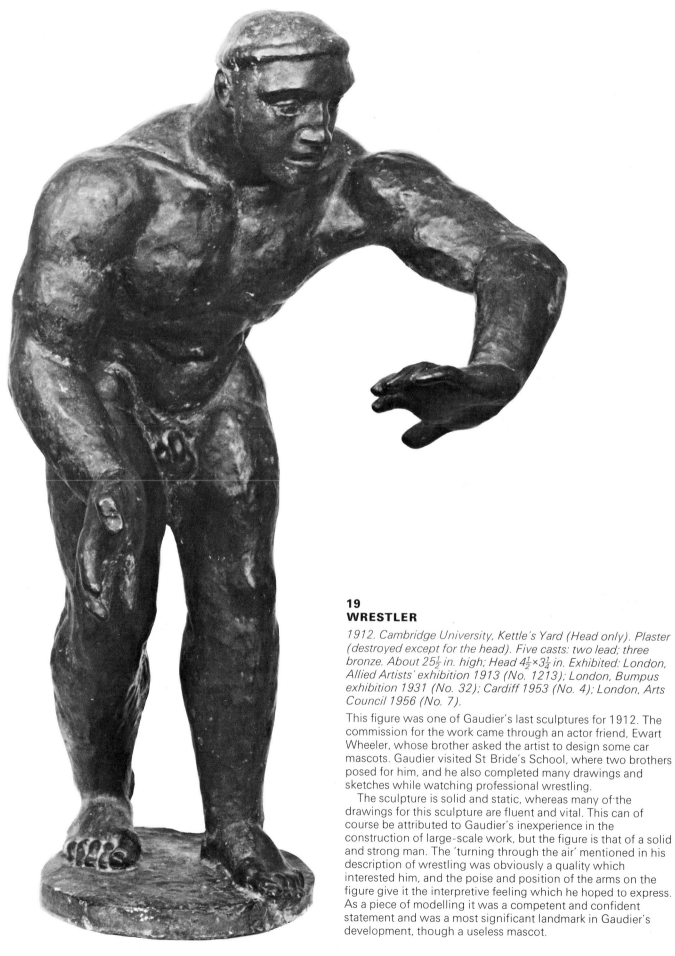

19
WRESTLER

1912. Cambridge University, Kettle's Yard (Head only). Plaster (destroyed except for the head). Five casts: two lead; three bronze. About 25½ in. high; Head 4½×3¼ in. Exhibited: London, Allied Artists' exhibition 1913 (No. 1213); London, Bumpus exhibition 1931 (No. 32); Cardiff 1953 (No. 4); London, Arts Council 1956 (No. 7).

This figure was one of Gaudier's last sculptures for 1912. The commission for the work came through an actor friend, Ewart Wheeler, whose brother asked the artist to design some car mascots. Gaudier visited St Bride's School, where two brothers posed for him, and he also completed many drawings and sketches while watching professional wrestling.

The sculpture is solid and static, whereas many of the drawings for this sculpture are fluent and vital. This can of course be attributed to Gaudier's inexperience in the construction of large-scale work, but the figure is that of a solid and strong man. The 'turning through the air' mentioned in his description of wrestling was obviously a quality which interested him, and the poise and position of the arms on the figure give it the interpretive feeling which he hoped to express. As a piece of modelling it was a competent and confident statement and was a most significant landmark in Gaudier's development, though a useless mascot.

20 PORTRAIT OF HORACE BRODZKY

1913. Cambridge University, Kettle's Yard. Portland stone (relief). Nine casts in artificial stone. 14 ×15 in. Exhibited: Edinburgh, Scottish National Gallery of Modern Art 1972 (No. 18).

The carving is of particular interest because it forms a link with three aspects of the artist's work, namely, the *Ornamental Mask* (No. 4), the relief stone carvings such as *Woman* (No. 11) and the portrait bust of Horace Brodzky (No. 21).

The sculpture was unrecognized until 1971, when the author related it to entries in Gaudier's *List of Works*: 'Brodzky masque prime portland graneur nature,' and a letter to Sophie, 'There are certainly a few of the remaining sculptures we should be glad to see housed elsewhere . . . the stone head of Brodzky.'[1]

1. Letter from Leicester Galleries to Sophie 25.10.1918.

. PORTRAIT OF HORACE BRODZKY

1913. Cambridge, Mass., Fogg Museum. Plaster painted pale green. Six bronze casts. 23¾×21 in. Exhibited: London, Allied Artists'
exhibition 1913 (No. 1216); London, Bumpus exhibition 1931 (No. 38); Glasgow, Institute of Fine Arts 1931 (No. 59); Leeds
1943 (No. 67); Orléans 1956 (No. 13); London, Arts Council 1956 (No. 19); Edinburgh, Gallery of Modern Art 1972 (No. 19).

This portrait, together with the *Portrait of Alfred Wolmark* (No. 22), is of particular importance in the development of Gaudier's
sculpture. The assurance and almost arrogant determination of these two heads are a culmination of many of the earlier searches of
1912 and express a definite determination on the part of the sculptor to portray the outstanding characteristics of his two friends.
Helped by the freedom of the situation (he was not working for a commission), the sculptor had a far greater opportunity of
expressing his real beliefs. Consequently these heads are Gaudier's most positive application of Cubist beliefs. It can only be
assumed that he had learnt much of the Cubist thinking through his contact with Epstein, but Epstein could not have described a
Cubist style in sculpture since the best-known sculpture, Picasso's 1909 *Head of a Woman*, was a three-dimensional
interpretation of a painting. Gaudier's sculptural interpretation of Cubism is therefore more closely related to the geometric Cubist
paintings of the period before 1910 and not to Analytical Cubism, which followed it. In his searchings for an expressive approach
to sculpture in 1912 Gaudier had almost anticipated the present work, which makes it far more acceptable as a natural development.

 In both sculptures there is a deliberate exaggeration of the geometric planes generally more developed in the Brodzky bust. All
the earlier enquiries into a variety of styles seem to anticipate these works and they were undoubtedly seen by the artist as an
important step forward. When these sculptures were exhibited in July 1913 they caused an uproar in the Press, and Gaudier was
termed 'recklessly defiant' in his presentation 'of fierce uncouth versions of the human encumberance', calculated to attract
attention only and failing to convey a 'sense of the sitter's character and appearance.'

 The sculpture appears in Gaudier's *List of Works*: 'donne Horace Brodzky, Herne Hill cubique.'

22
PORTRAIT OF ALFRED WOLMARK

*1913. Liverpool, Walker Art Gallery.
Plaster. Six bronze casts. $26\frac{1}{2} \times 21\frac{1}{2}$ in.
Exhibited: London, Allied Artists'
exhibition 1913 (No. 1217).*

See the note to the portrait head of
Horace Brodzky (No. 21). If anything,
this portrait is even more purposeful
than the Brodzky portrait. The posture
of the head turned at right-angles to
the chest gives the whole sculpture a
surprisingly arrogant posture when
seen at eye level. More daring
therefore in its concept than the
Brodzky bust, this sculpture is equally
significant and was a major advance
for the artist.

The sculpture appears in Gaudier's
List of Works: 'donne Al. Wolmark,
47 Broadhurst Gdns. cubique.'

23
RELIGIOUS HEAD

*About 1912/13. Cambridge
University, Kettle's Yard (stolen 1977).
White marble. Twelve casts in bronze.
5 ×2½ in. Exhibited: Orléans 1956
(No. 3).*

The inscription on the reverse almost
certainly refers to the estranged
friendship of Gaudier (P) and Sophie
(Z) with Murry (M) and Mansfield (K).
The work is not significant and holds
little importance in the artist's
developing style, being more likely to
be part of those sculptures created as
toys or for friends rather than a serious
work.

24. PORTRAIT OF POUND

1912/13. Private collection. Marble. No casts known. 5 ×3¾ in. Exhibited: London, Fine Arts Society 1968.

This sculpture which is similar in size to *Religious Head* (No. 23) is also reminiscent of it in style. Like *Religious Head* the carving is not a fully developed three-dimensional sculpture and must be regarded as one of Gaudier's early exploratory works. The visual resemblance to Ezra Pound in this carving is slight and it may be that the name of the sculpture was added in later years to make it appear more significant.

Below
Maillol: *Seated Nude.*

25. SEPULCHRAL FIGURE

1913. London, Tate Gallery. Bath stone. Four bronze casts, at least. 16 × 14½ in.
Exhibited: London, Memorial exhibition 1918 (No. 89); Leeds 1943 (No. 65); Orléans
1956 (No. 2); London, Arts Council 1956 (No. 8); Edinburgh, Scottish National Gallery
of Modern Art 1972 (No. 21).

This stone carving has a distinct relationship with Maillol's sculptures of 1901 to 1909,
particularly *Night* (1902–5) and *Mediterranean* (1901). Although there is no evidence
that this work was directly derivative from Maillol's work, the similarity cannot be
overlooked. Perhaps the soft roundness, which is evident in this sculpture and in later
female forms, can also be attributed to Maillol's influence. This sculpture is therefore
exploratory, it is the earliest example of the artist's work where the stone block has been
opened up, and there is also a feeling in the work, as in earlier carvings, of the figure
being fitted into the stone. The sculpture looks unfinished, being particularly
inconclusive in the similarity of the treatment of the pedestal and hair. This can be
accounted for by remembering Gaudier's relative lack of skill and experience in handling
stone, but it is interesting to consider how rapidly these skills were acquired when
comparing this work with later sculptures of the same year. In contrast to the first stone
heads, supposedly cut for Epstein's benefit a year earlier, this sculpture shows that even
with such little opportunity to interpret his ideas in stone, Gaudier's realization as a
sculptor had taken a step forward.

Exchanged with Alfred Wolmark in return for a portrait of himself[1] this sculpture
appears in Gaudier's *List of Works*. The sculpture was sold in the 1950s, incorrectly
attributed to Maillol.

1. Orléans, Musée des Beaux Arts.

26. DOG

1913. Chicago, Art Institute. Marble, painted. No casts known. 9½×19 in.

The carving of the dog is not an important work and may be regarded as a three-dimensional interpretation of a drawing. There is, however, in its interpretation into stone an interesting simplification of the original drawing and a concern to establish lines of movement within the figure. The limited depth of stone obviously presented problems with overlapping forms.

The sculpture undoubtedly fits into a category of work which reflects earlier painted stone and plaster sculpture and was probably designed as a saleable piece.

In 1916 the carving was owned by Frank Harris. To date there has been no evidence found that he purchased the work from Gaudier during his lifetime, although this would have been possible. It was acquired by the Art Institute of Chicago from the John Quinn collection.

27
FEMALE FIGURE

1913. Manchester, City Art Gallery.
Alabaster. No casts known. 14¾×7¼ in.
Exhibited: Edinburgh, Scottish
National Gallery of Modern Art 1972.

Gaudier carved this sculpture in the
early part of 1913 and it anticipates
developments of style and form in later
sculptures. It is particularly interesting
to notice the stylized treatment of the
face and hair, which is a development
from some of the earlier carvings of
1912, such as *Man and Woman*
(No. 12). Of particular interest also is
the position of the arms behind the
back, a design problem at this stage
and later developed in another carving
The Singer (No. 28). The soft
roundness of the earlier *Sepulchral*
Figure (No. 25) is also present in this
work and it is interesting to compare
this sculpture with the later *Torsos*
(Nos 29, 31), which show a more
advanced understanding of the form
and greater sympathy with the stone.

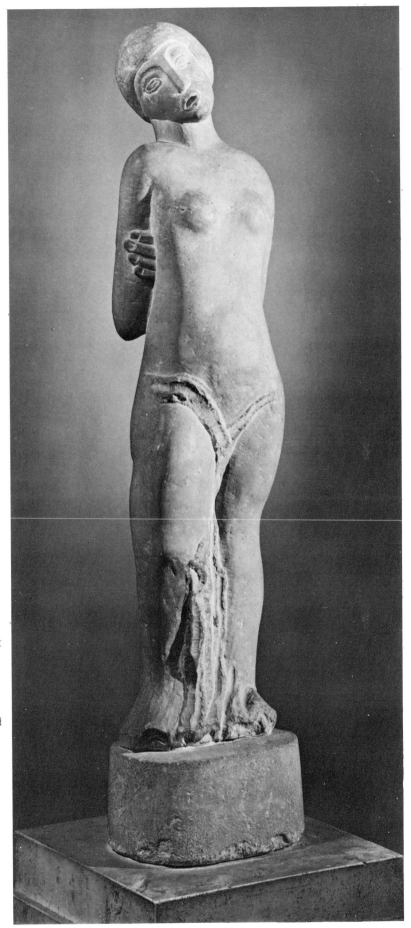

28
SINGER

1913. London, Tate Gallery. Derby stone. No casts. 33½×8½ in. Exhibited: London, Goupil Gallery 1915 (No. 95); London, Vorticists exhibition, Doré Gallery 1915 (No. e); London, Memorial exhibition 1918 (No. 100); Leeds, Temple Newsam 1943 (No. 64); London, Arts Council 1956 (No. 17).

This sculpture was Gaudier's first major carving to exceed twelve inches in height. The ambition which he had expressed earlier to Dr Uhlemayr was now realized, but at the same time he found himself involved in problems of carving which he was inadequately trained to overcome. At first sight this carving would appear to be directly influenced by early Greek sculpture, but the interpretation of the figure, above the waist, incorporates his best understanding of the simplification of forms. Below the waist there are unresolved and foreshortened areas which suggest a mixture of classical and the primitive, and these unsatisfactorily complete the figure. The stylized treatment of the hair and folded arms behind the back of the figure is a new concept which is not anticipated in any earlier work other than the *Female Figure* (No. 27). The treatment of the hand and the hair together show a sensitive expression of this new concern for the simplification of forms and reveal a new dimension in Gaudier's understanding and ability. For the first time in this carving, as opposed to working in clay, he moves quite obviously away from a primary concern for realistic representation. The quality of the stone must have presented particular problems to Gaudier and many of the point-marks left on this carving were probably the result of his lack of suitable chisels for handling the harder stone, as well as lack of skill.

This sculpture appears in Gaudier's *List of Works*: 'Chanteuse statuette pierre duse Derby 2½ in. haut.'

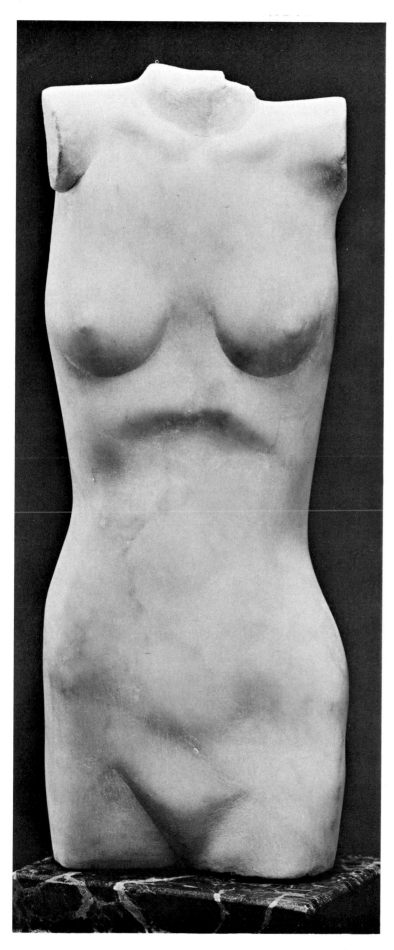

29
FEMALE TORSO 1

1913. London, Victoria and Albert Museum. Grey veined white marble. No casts. 10 ×3 in. Exhibited: London, Goupil Gallery 1914 (No. 115); London, Memorial exhibition 1918 (No. 8); Edinburgh, Scottis National Gallery of Modern Art 1972 (No. 23).

Recorded by Gaudier in his *List of Works* as 'a portrait of Nina Hamnett, painter.' This torso, with two others, reveals an outstanding ability not previously realized i the artist's work. The sculptures show that the artist d in fact understand and assimilate much of his earlier observations of classical works of art. There is a sensuous delight in the translation of this figure into marble, and Gaudier shows in this work that he could handle form in 'the accepted manner', and consequently justifies earlier years spent in the study c other artists. This sculpture is the work of an accomplished stone carver in the grand manner. Long before this sculpture was completed, Gaudier wrote, 'I long to make a statue of a single body, an absolutely truthful copy — something so true that it will whe it is made.' Here is the realization of that aspiration.

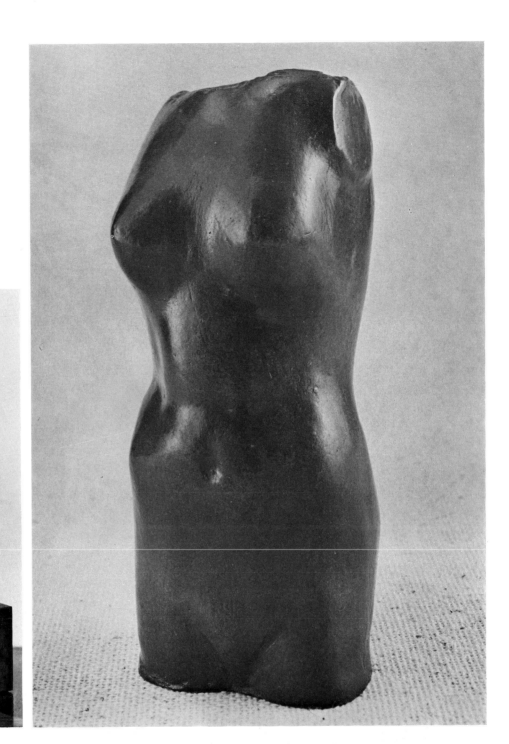

30. FEMALE TORSO 2

1913. Clay. Clay model probably destroyed, from which two plasters were cast. Five casts, three with chipped breast. $8\frac{1}{4} \times 3\frac{1}{2}$ in. Exhibited: London, Memorial exhibition 1918 (No. 8).

Often confused with *Torso 1* (No. 29); although similar to it, this *Torso* is in fact a different sculpture. Gaudier made a clay model from which two plasters were cast; the clay model and one plaster were given to Alfred Wolmark, and the second plaster, which had one breast damaged, was given to Horace Brodzky. Five bronzes have been cast from Wolmark's plaster, at least three from the Brodzky plaster. Much confusion still surrounds the whereabouts and numbering of these bronzes.

Modelled by Nina Hamnett (see also Nos 29, 31), Gaudier wrote to Major Smythies, 'a statue of a girl in a natural way in order to show my accomplishment as a sculptor . . . We are of different opinions about naturalism. I treat it as a hollow accomplishment, the artificial is full of metaphysical meaning which is all important.'[1]

1. Major Smythies quoting Gaudier in a letter to H. S. Ede. 1929. Private collection.

31. FEMALE TORSO 3

About 1913/14. Italy, Ezra Pound collection. Marble. No casts known. 9×3 in.
Exhibited: London, Memorial exhibition 1918 (No. 18); Milan 1957 (No. 8).

The notes to Nos 29 and 30 provide background information to this sculpture, which
was owned by Mrs Shakespeare and later by Ezra Pound until his death. The sculpture
appears in Gaudier's *List of Works* as 'Torso de femme, marbre Seravezza 7 in. haut £10.
Mrs O. Shakespeare Portrait de Nina Hamnette peintre.'

Rodin: *Invocation.* Paris, Musée Rodin

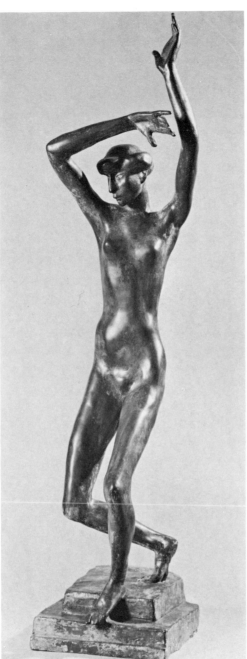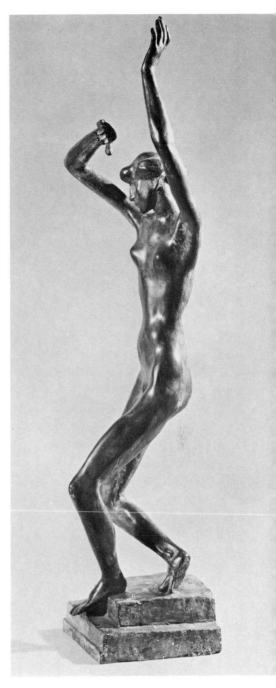

32. DANCER

1913. London, Tate Gallery. Plaster. Seven bronze casts. 31 ×7¼ in. Exhibited: London, Memorial exhibition 1918.

Noted in Gaudier's *List of Works*, this sculpture causes a confusion in the appreciation of his development, having been created in the middle of 1913 when the artist's development seemed set toward abstraction. The return to a more realistic representation in this sculpture and the *Torsos*, Nos 29, 30, 31, was adequately explained by Gaudier in the letter to his patron Major Smythies, already quoted.

I am working 'a statue of a girl in a natural way in order to show my accomplishment as a sculptor . . . We are of different opinions about naturalism, I treat it as a hollow accomplishment. . . .'

This sculpture and the torsos are of the same period. The *Dancer*, said by Horace Brodzky to have been posed for by Sophie Brzeska, achieves a level of expression which is completely original. The whole figure is poised in motion, and contains a spiral, rhythm and balance, all as integral parts of a captured moment. Earlier in 1912 Gaudier Brzeska had been enthusiastic about Rodin's sculptural objectives relating to movement; this work shows that not only had he understood them but could express it by creating works which expressed 'the transition of movement'. To Mrs Schiff, for whom the sculpture was created, the artist wrote, 'It is a sincere expression of a certain disposition of my mind, but you must know it is by no means the simplest nor the last.'

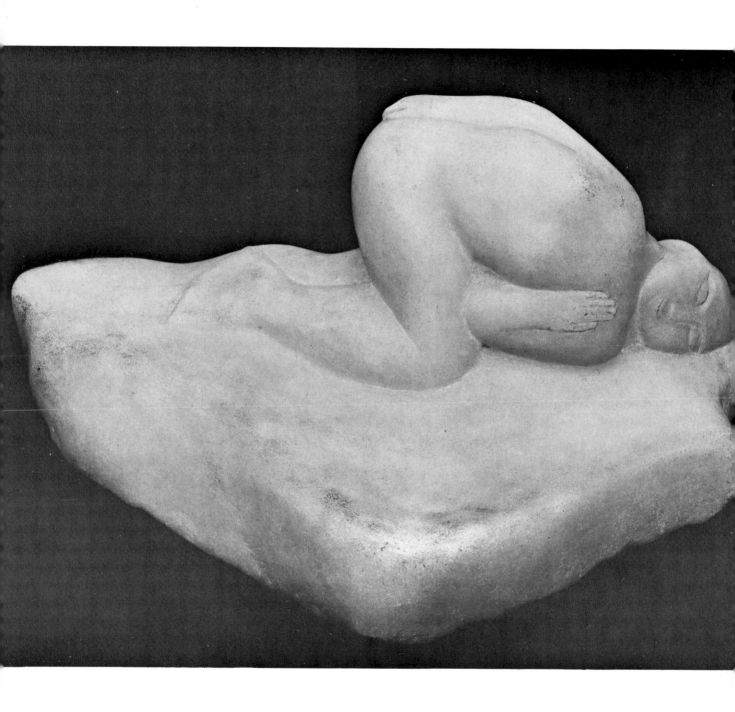

33. MERMAID

1913. Cambridge University, Kettle's Yard. Marble. Nine casts in bronze. $4\frac{1}{2} \times 7\frac{1}{4}$ in. Exhibited: London, Bumpus exhibition 1931 (No. 34); Leeds 1943 (No. 74); Cardiff 1953 (No. 9); Orléans 1956 (No. 6); London, Arts Council 1956 (No. 22); Edinburgh, Scottish National Gallery of Modern Art 1972 (No. 27).

Undoubtedly influenced by Rodin's *Danaid*, this sculpture is an important step in the artist's development. Particularly noticeable is the treatment of the head and hands which are abstracted more positively in this than in any previous work. The response to the quality of the surface of the marble is also important. Following Rodin and Michelangelo he tried to achieve a feeling of the figure emerging from the stone block.

This is the last significant carving of 1913 which shows direct stylistic influences and it is also the key to much of the abstract development of the figure which took place in 1914.

odin: *Danaïd*. 1885. Paris, Musée Rodin.

34. MATERNITY

1913. Paris, Musée d'Art Moderne. Polished Seravezza marble. Eight bronze casts.
$11 \times 10\frac{1}{4}$ *in. Exhibited: London, Goupil Gallery 1914 (No. 111); London, Whitechapel*
1914 (No. 156); London, Memorial exhibition 1918 (No. 35); London, Bumpus
exhibition 1931 (No. 35).

The stone for this work came from the Omega workshops, and consequently the
sculpture shows none of the peculiar limitations of many earlier works carved from odd
blocks of stone. The sculpture is complete, rounded and rhythmic; the broad treatment
of the planes of the group are coherent and have the solidarity of Maillol's figures, yet
flow consistently. The two figures are compact and strong and this solidity has been
achieved by an arrangement of the proportions of the figure which produce well-
balanced simplified masses. In many ways this sculpture bridges the gap between the
Torsos (Nos 29, 30, 31) and later work; it shows all the accomplishments of an
experienced sculptor but is unique in its proportions, inherent strength and feeling for
the subject. In understanding Gaudier's development towards the abstract, this work is
significant in that it embodies many new ideas and simplifies many of his earlier
Maillol–Rodin problems through a directness of interpretation. It was in sculptures
around this time that Gaudier found opportunity to express many of his earlier theories
about the relationship of planes and masses, and in late 1913 he was developing more
rapidly than ever before. *Maternity* appears in Gaudier's *List of Works* as 'to be sold by
the Omega workshops for £20, one quarter of which was commission.'

35. CROUCHING FIGURE

1913. Minneapolis, Walker Art Center. White marble. No casts. 8¾×12 ×4 in. Exhibited: Orléans 1956 (No. 12); London, Arts Council 1956 (No. 10); Edinburgh, Scottish National Gallery of Modern Art 1972 (No. 28).

This carving was probably started by Gaudier in 1913 and completed in 1914. Little is known about the work before December 1955, when it was purchased in London. Some confusion has been caused by the title of the work, but it seems most likely that this sculpture is in fact that described by the artist as a 'Relief Carving, of Seravezza marble, 10 ×4 in. Sold to Renee Finch for 18/–'. The interrelationship of forms in this work are a direct development from earlier carvings of the female form, such as *Maternity* (No. 34). As in that sculpture, Gaudier was preoccupied with the interrelationship of forms, but, in addition, this work shows a flowing movement from one form to another and the concern for design, in places, takes over from realistic representation.

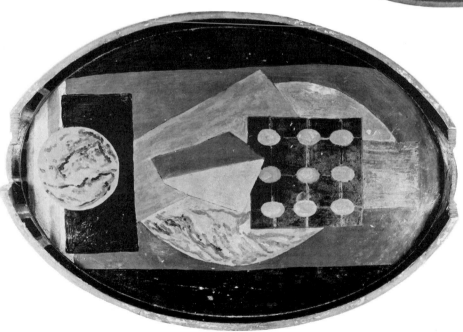

36
TWO TRAYS

1913. London, Victoria and Albert Museum, and private collection. Both inlaid and painted wood. No casts known. No. 1, about 25 in. diameter; No. 2, about 25 ×17 in. oval. Exhibited: London, Memorial exhibition 1918 (No. 102).

During his employment at the Omega workshops Gaudier made two trays, the first of which is an adaptation of one of his drawings of dancing figures; the other is an experiment in the abstract forms.

The design was dictated in both these trays by the standard shapes used in the Omega workshops. It is important to note that the abstraction in the design of the fingers and toes of the dancing figures is a development from the treatment of hands in *Mermaid* (No. 33). Since the trays were made at the Omega workshops, neither appears in Gaudier's *List of Works.*

37. CAT

1913. Bristol, City Art Gallery, and other collections. Fired and glazed ceramic. Four fired clay casts in various glazes known. 5 ×4 in. Exhibited: London, Arts Council 1956 (No. 18).

The *Cat* is a realistic three-dimensional interpretation reflecting many of Gaudier's pen and pencil studies of his own cat, given to him by Spencer Gore. In his modelling of the subject there is a definite reflection of oriental influences, but the treatment of the surfaces and their relationships gives this work a commercial flavour. The casts, at least four of which are known to survive, were glazed and fired in the Omega workshops in cream, black, dark blue and brown, and as a consequence of the poor quality of the glazing the whole work is inconclusive.

Opposite:

38. STATUETTE OF A BOY

About 1913. Devon, Dartington Hall. Alabaster. 46.9 in. high. Two bronze casts known. Exhibited: London, Alpine Gallery 1914 (No. 46); London, Arts Council 1956 (No. 11); Stadt Bielefeld 1969 (No. 7, bronze); Edinburgh, Scottish National Gallery of Modern Art 1972 (No. 29).

This alabaster was also completed at the Omega workshops (see Nos 36, 37). Being short of money, the opportunity for large and well proportioned stone which did not limit the shape of his sculptures appealed to Gaudier. This carving is not so strong as some of the artist's other figure studies of 1913; it has a soft rounded appearance and lacks the vital strength and expression which is present in figures like *The Dancer* (No. 32). How far the rounded softness can be attributed to the qualities of the stone, it is difficult to assess, but the figure also has characteristic qualitites repeated in carvings such as *Red Stone Dancer*, particularly the foreshortening of the legs and position of the arms in relation to the head. *Red Stone Dancer* shows substantial developments from this work, which underlines how the problems of abstract geometric design were still, at this stage, not completely understood.

The sculpture appears in Gaudier's *List of Works*: 'Garçon statuette, alabâtre.'

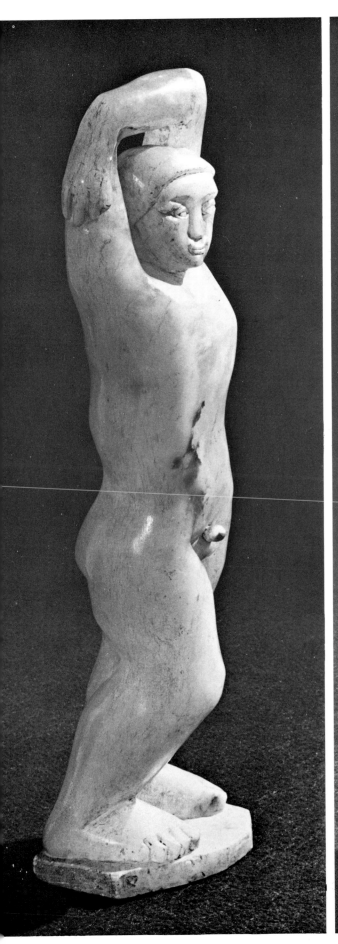
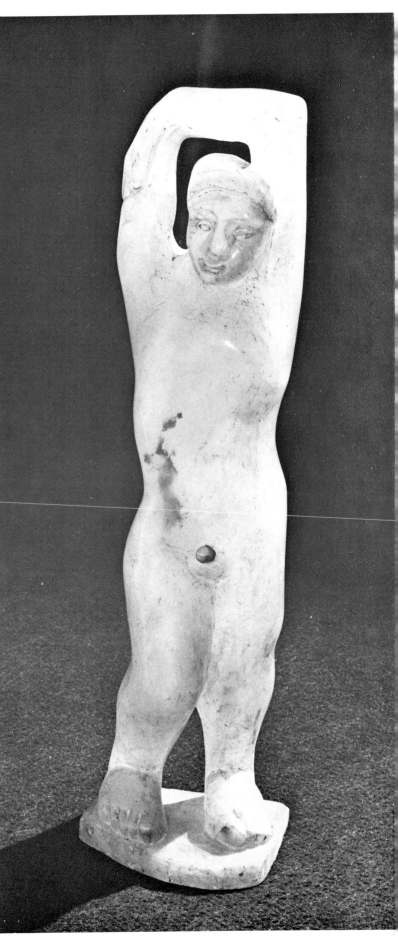

39. SLEEPING FAWN

1913. Private collection. Polished Seravezza marble. Twelve casts in bronze. 6 ×5 in. Exhibited: London, Memorial exhibition 1918 (No. 98, lent by O. Raymond Drey).

This fawn, not to be confused with Nos 47 and 48 *(Fawn Crouching)*, is one of a number of realistic animal studies which Gaudier created in spare moments and often gave as presents to friends. He also enjoyed making models of cats and dogs, and these too were frequently given away. Although these sculptures were created in a less serious vein, they do reveal a great deal of the artist's real character, and when later in 1913 and 1914 these 'toys' became more abstract, they in turn show that even when playing with ideas in small pieces of stone or clay Gaudier was thinking intuitively in semi-abstract terms.

The sculpture appears in Gaudier's *List of Works*: 'Faon statuette marbre Seravezza' and was sold by him for £5. 0. 0. to Raymond Drey, from whom its provenance can readily be traced.

40. CROUCHING FAWN

1913. London, Tate Gallery. Plaster painted light brown. Twelve casts in bronze.
4¼×10 in. Exhibited: Edinburgh, Scottish National Gallery of Modern Art 1972 (No. 30).

Not to be confused with No. 39, the casts from this plaster are different in both design and size, but similar to *Fawn Crouching* (No. 48), a stone carving worked to the design of this plaster.

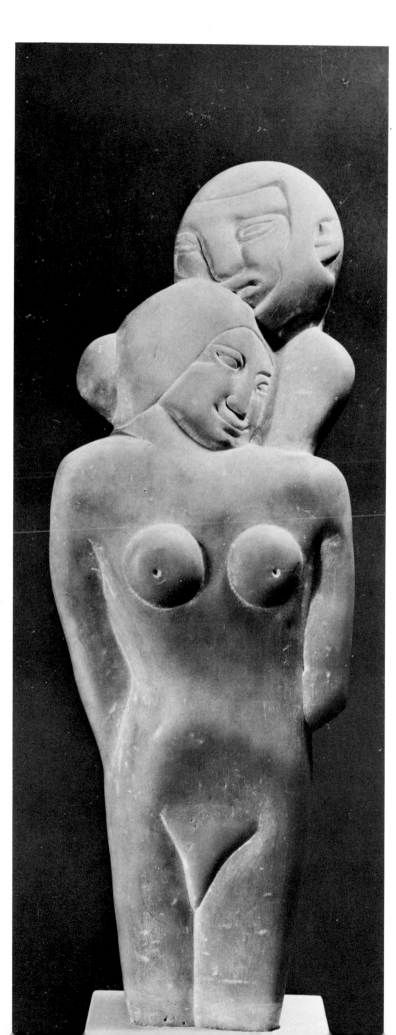

41
EMBRACERS (Samson and Delilah)

*Late 1913 or 1914. Paris, Musée d'Art Moderne.
Marble. Three casts in plaster, two in bronze.
21½×7½ in. Exhibited: London, Memorial exhibition
1918 (No. 39).*

This sculpture is important in Gaudier's chronological
development if compared with his earlier attempts at
developing an abstract form, as for instance in the
alabaster figure of the boy (No. 38). It is a sculpture
which, like *Singer* (No. 28), has specific problems in
relation to the proportion of the stone, and Gaudier
handled this problem, as with *Crouching Figure*
(No. 35) with particular skill by treating the carving
almost as a two-dimensional relief.

Pound, in his list of works, describes the carving as
follows: 'Marble group, man and woman, (?)
Tahitian. At least one might so regard its ancestry
were it not one of Gaudier's most personal
expressions. The faces do, I think, suggest some
Oceanic tradition, the right arm of the woman is most
delicate in its straightness, and suggests that of a
certain Isis with Horus between her knees (green
stone, British Museum).'[1]

Pound's theory is helpful in determining how this
occurred, seemingly out of sequence, and although
Pound's theory may be accurate, Gaudier certainly
had explored problems such as the simplification of
the face in works like *Singer* (No. 28).

But this work is unique in the development of this
interpretation in areas such as the treatment of the
line of hair, and the ears on the male figure. There is a
great deal of similarity between the frontal design of
the female figure in this carving and *Singer*, but it
does show a considerable abstract development from
Singer as, for example, in the basic treatment of the
breasts.

This sculpture, which appears in Gaudier's *List of
Works*, is described as 'Samson and Delilah.
Saravezza Marble 1¾' haut circa groupe erotique. £5.
Ezra Pound 5 Holland Place Kensington.'

1. Pound, 1, p. 159.

42. THE WRESTLERS

1914. Boston, Mass., Museum of Fine Arts. Plaster. Nine casts in Herculite. 28½×36¼ in. Exhibited: London, Memorial exhibition 1918 (No. 69); Leeds 1943 (No. 78); London, Arts Council 1956 (No. 28).

This plaster relief was modelled directly on the reverse side of an earlier oil painting on canvas, *Portrait of a Jew*, 'a Whitechapel Jew selling trash.'[1]

The relief was the culmination of a large number of drawings on this subject which gradually became more simplified. The treatment is essentially two-dimensional and is concerned to establish a rhythmic interrelation of shapes. The flat treatment of the hands, which is a further progression from earlier expressions of the same form, serve to accentuate the flow of lines in the two figures. There is little development of style in the design of the two heads, in comparison with the *Embracers* (No. 41), but what is quite evident is that the proportion and natural physical organization of the figure has been abandoned entirely in favour of the direct expression of the interrelationships of the subject. Consequently this work established a further step towards an original means of expression, in which the drawing and sculpture were one.

This work appears in Gaudier's *List of Works*: 'Lutteurs bas relief platre 3'0 ×2'5 Modelage direct en platre.'

1. Sophie's diary. Essex University Library.

43. RED STONE DANCER

1914. London, Tate Gallery. Red Mansfield stone. One bronze cast. 17 ×9 in. Exhibited: London, Alpine Gallery 1914 (No. 50); London, Goupil Gallery 1914 (No 113); London, Vorticists exhibition 1915 (No. c); London, Memorial exhibition 1918 (No. 72); Leeds 1943 (No. 75); Orléans 1956 (No. 14); London, Arts Council 1956 (No. 24); Edinburgh, Scottish National Gallery of Modern Art 1972 (No. 32); Eastbourne Art Gallery 1977.

Like *Crouching Figure* (No. 35), this sculpture was probably started in 1913 and completed in 1914. Unlike the earlier *Dancer* of 1913 (No. 32), this work is uncompromising, simplified and direct. The movement within the structure of the figure, the foreshortening of the legs, the position of the arm and its relationship to the head and body, all show developments from problems explored in earlier experiments. This sculpture extends the artist's language of abstraction and we find new forms and designs in the expression of the face, breasts and hands. This work is a positive development of the earlier explorations and the sculpture achieves completely original statements. Describing this sculpture Ezra Pound wrote: 'This is almost a thesis of his ideas upon the use of pure form. We have the triangle and circle asserted, *labled* [sic] almost, upon the face and right breast. Into these so-called 'abstractions' life flows, the circle moves and elongates into the oval, it increases and takes volume in the sphere, or hemisphere of the breast. The triangle moves toward organism, it becomes spherical triangle (the central life-form common to both Brzeska and Lewis). These two developed motifs work as themes in a fugue. We have the whole series of spherical triangles, as in the arm over the head, all combining and culminating in the great sweep of the back of the shoulders, as fine as any surface in all sculpture. The 'abstract' or mathematical bareness of the triangle and circle are fully incarnate, made flesh, full of vitality and of energy. The whole form-series ends, passes into stasis with the circular base or platform.'[1]

 The sculpture appears in Gaudier's *List of Works* as 'Danseuse statuette gris rouge Mansfield, Poli a la cise.'

1. Pound, 2, pp. 37–8, not with reference to No. 32 as stated in Tate Gallery Catalogue British School 1964.

Red Stone Dancer (No. 43)

44. MATERNITY (Also known as CHARITY)

1914. Orléans, Musée des Beaux Arts. Portland stone. Two casts known in artificial stone. 17¾×8 in. Exhibited: London, Vorticist exhibition 1915 (No. 156); Leeds 1943 (No. 76); Orléans 1956 (No. 8); London, Arts Council 1956 (No. 20).

In Gaudier's *List of Works* this sculpture is named 'Maternité groupe. Pierre Portland 3 figures.'

The mother figure in this carving is a direct development of the abstraction in *Red Stone Dancer* (No. 43) and it is really the texture of the surface in this carving which exaggerates the differences between the two sculptures. Once again the interplay of the arms and head form an exciting composition, and the head repeats, with an incised line, the triangular design from the head of the *Red Stone Dancer*.

The design of this sculpture is particularly interesting, with the mass of the stone supported by the trunks of the three figures. Surprisingly, the head and arms seem uplifted, rather than weighted, and this must be due to the tension created in the upward thrust of the two children and the contrasting rhythmic movement of the shape of the back of the mother.

45
VASE (STATUETTE)

1913/14. Ezra Pound collection, Brunnenburg. Sicilian marble. No cast. About 17 in high. Exhibited: London, Alpine Gallery 1914 (No. 45).

This sculpture appears in Gaudier's *List of Works* as 'Vase statuette marbre Seravezza $1\frac{1}{2} \times 2 \times 3\frac{1}{4}$ comm Omega.'

Carved in stone obtained from the Omega workshops, and purchased from them by Ezra Pound for John Quinn in 1916 together with *Cat* (No. 46), this work has not been seen by the author except in photographs. The abstract nature of the work, together with references to it by Gaudier, date this work as 1913/14. It was described by Pound in 1914 as *Water Carrier* and this description is conveyed in the nature of the work.

46. CAT

1914. P.B. de Rachelwiltz, Ezra Pound collection, Brunnenburg. Seravezza marble. No casts. 9 ×17 in. Exhibited: London, Alpine Gallery 1914 (No. 49); London, Whitechapel Gallery 1914 (No. 188).

This sculpture is detailed in Gaudier's *List of Works*, but like No. 45 has been in a private collection since 1916, and never exhibited since. It is a typical example of Gaudier's ability at fitting his subject within the material whilst displaying intricate interrelationships of shape. Semi-abstract in interpretation, this carving is one of his less serious works.

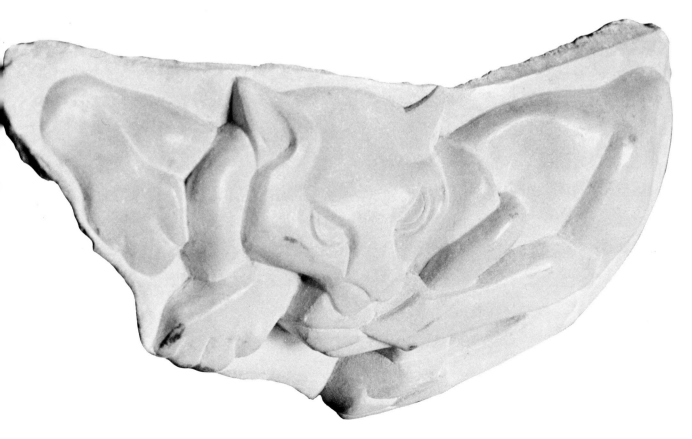

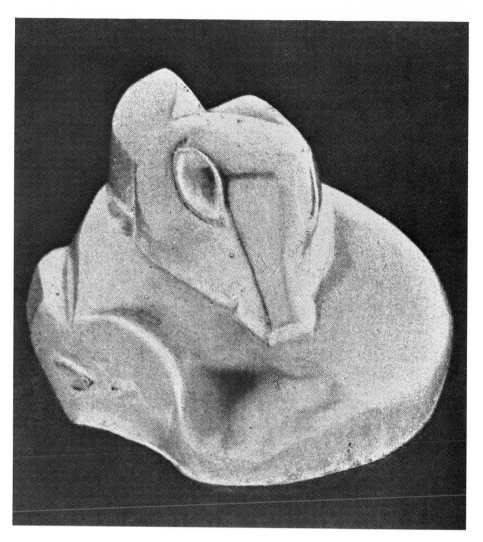

47. FAWN CROUCHING

1914. P.B. de Rachelwiltz, Ezra Pound collection, Brunnenburg. Bath stone. One bronze cast known. 3 × 2 in. Exhibited: London, Memorial exhibition 1918 (No. 17).

Dated by Gaudier in his *List of Works* as 1914, sold to 'Mrs. E. Pound Kensington for £1. 10. 0. enduite de resine.' (See also notes to Nos 39, 40, 48.)

48. FAWN CROUCHING

1914. Private collection. Bath stone. One plaster and at least twelve bronze casts. 12 × 10 in. Exhibited: London, Memorial exhibition 1918 (No. 96); London, Bumpus exhibition 1931 (No. 39).

Dated by Gaudier to 1914 and sold for '£15 − $\frac{1}{4}$ comm Omega to Mrs Major Campden Hill.' (See notes to Nos 39, 40, 47.) Not illustrated in this book.

49. CASKET

1914. Private collection. Marble. No casts. 6 × 12 in.

This casket is detailed in the artist's *List of Works* and he was paid £6. 0. 0. for carving it. It must be regarded as a commercial piece of work which adds little to our understanding of the artist.

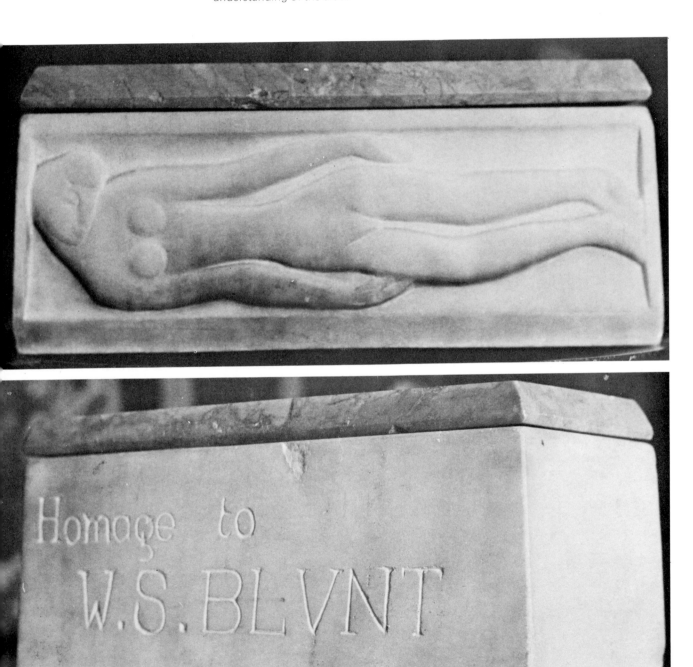

50
HIERATIC HEAD OF EZRA POUND

1914. Ezra Pound collection. Marble. No casts. 36 ×24 in. Exhibited: London, Whitechapel Gallery 1914 (No. 154).

Responding to the challenge both of the material and the idea, Gaudier created a unique carving in this sculpture. Gaudier had continually told Pound: 'It will not look like you, it will . . . not . . . look . . . like you. It will be the expression of certain emotions which I got from your character.'[1] But Pound was ecstatic about the completed carving. A number of photographs were taken, with obvious pride, during work on the head, and Gaudier being photographed with his subject in the process of its development has not only helped to provide accurate dating of the work, but it has also enabled models to be attributed to Gaudier's studio by the author. This recording process was used on a number of occasions by Gaudier in 1914, the photographer being Walter Bennington, a friend of Haldane Macfall, whom Gaudier introduced to Pound.

In its final form the Pound head adequately interpreted its objectives, and because of its massive size and presence had echoes of monumental ritual carvings which may in truth have been one of the many motivating forces behind its design. As the last portrait head it stands as a landmark in Gaudier's development, proving that he had shaken himself free of earlier academic ideas, and in portrait sculpture was coming near to an original style.

1. Pound, 1, p. 52.

Henri Gaudier in his studio working on the *Hieratic Head*.

51
PORTRAIT OF EZRA POUND

1914. Yale, University Art Gallery. Wood. No casts known. 28¾ in. high. Base 6¾×6¾×1½ in.

This carving is unique in Gaudier's work and there has consequently been some speculation as to its authenticity. The work is not mentioned in the artist's *List of Works* nor is it detailed in the list of sculptures which Pound took into safe keeping before Gaudier left for the trenches. However, the provenance of the carving is well documented and the style of the carving is closely related to other sculptures, particularly *Men with Bowl* (No. 59). This sculpture is similarly a very derivative carving but does overcome the problem of the arrangement of geometric forms in a rhythmic and flowing sculptural form. This carving has certain similarities with the *Hieratic Head* of Ezra Pound (No. 50) and it is quite likely that whilst the stone took many weeks to complete; this totemic carving was done quickly as a physical expression of Pound, reflecting Gaudier's discussions on primitive art.

52. STAGS

1914. Chicago, Art Institute. Red-veined alabaster. No casts. 13¾×13½ in. Exhibited: London, Goupil Gallery 1914 (No. 112); London, Memorial exhibition 1918 (No. 44); London, Arts Council 1956 (No. 26); Edinburgh, Scottish National Gallery of Modern Art 1972 (No. 35).

This sculpture is yet another example of Gaudier's response to animals. Nina Hamnett recalled how, when she went for a walk with the artist in Richmond Park, 'he knew the antelopes', a description illustrating his real affinity with animal life. The treatment of the subject in this sculpture is far removed from the earlier Omega workshop sculptures such as the *Fawn Crouching* (No. 48). The simplification and interrelationship of shapes is more complicated than in *Red Stone Dancer* (No. 43), and later became more refined in sculptures such as *Dog* (No. 56). The rounded and planed masses of the sculpture are given more strength by the opening up of the stone block between the two forms, and the juxtaposition of the elevated planes act as a stimulating contrast to the lower rounded forms. It is also interesting to note the incised design of the eyes and the abstract interpretation of the animals' feet.

In Gaudier's *List of Works* he records that this work 'appeared in the first number of *Blast* and in *Sketch*, 25 March 1914'. This sculpture was acquired by the Art Institute of Chicago from the John Quinn collection.

53
BOY WITH A RABBIT

1914. S.W. de Rachelwiltz, Ezra Pound collection, Brunnenburg. Red-veined alabaster. No casts. 11 in. high. Exhibited: London, Goupil Gallery 1914 (No. 114); London, Allied Artists' exhibition 1914 (No. 1347); London, Vorticists exhibition 1915 (No. a); London, Memorial exhibition 1918 (No. 68).

Gaudier had been accepted as a member of the London Group at an election held on 15 February, where in competition with nine others he had been voted in by fifteen votes to three.[1] It would have been surprising had he not gained a place, since of the committee, Lewis, Epstein and Wadsworth were all his friends, and Gilman, Gore and Rutter supported him and were very influential.

This carving, which reverts back to the Brancusi-like simplification of the *Mermaid* for its treatment of the face, whilst using a similar expression of related masses to describe the legs, arms and hands, was reviewed by Gaudier in his criticism of the Allied Artists' Exhibition and referred to in his *List of Works.*

1. Voting paper. London Group. 7 Feb. 1914. Unpublished. Private collection.

54. GARDEN ORNAMENT 1 (Bird Bath)

1914. London, Mercury Gallery. Plaster. Two casts in two pieces, four casts in one piece. Without base $8\frac{5}{8}$ in. high. Base $10\frac{1}{2}\times10\frac{1}{2}\times2\frac{1}{2}$ in., signed and inscribed 'scale $\frac{1}{6}$ in.' Exhibited: London, Memorial exhibition 1918 (No. 103, a vase plaster). 20 March 1970, Christies, lot 147. Roger Fry, Anthony Fry, Mercury Gallery.

This sculpture was modelled at the Omega workshops and it is probable that it was a maquette for a commission, similar to *Garden Ornaments 2* and *3* although different in style. The sculpture is yet another example of Gaudier's interest in the caryatid form in sculpture and although a more representational interpretation of that idea, the sculpture shows his continued concern with the form of the figure in a continuous flowing line.

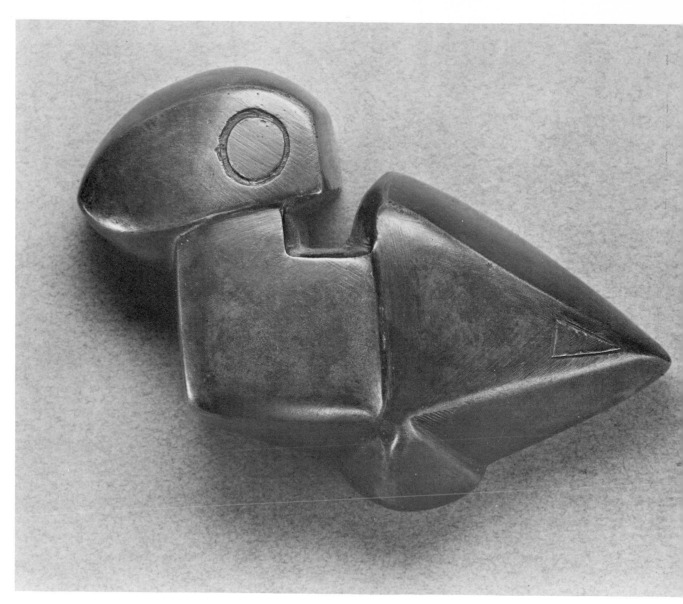

55. DUCK

1914. Cambridge University, Kettle's Yard. Marble. Twelve casts in bronze. Exhibited: Orléans 1956 (No. 5); London, Arts Council 1956 (No. 25).

Not included in Gaudier's *List of Works,* this small semi-abstract work is one of a number of small toys carved by Gaudier out of small pieces of stone for his friends.

56. DOG

1914. Private collection. Marble (damaged). One cast in aluminium, twelve in bronze. 6 ×13⅞ in. Exhibited: London, Bumpus exhibition 1931 (No. 40); Leeds 1943 (No. 73); Cardiff 1953 (No. 14); London, Arts Council 1956 (No. 23); London, Marlborough Gallery 1965 (No. 94).

This sculpture, sometimes referred to by Sophie Brzeska as 'Dachshound', combines serious study and sheer enjoyment. Unlike the *Fawns* of late 1913 and early 1914, which remained realistic in their representation, this sculpture retains the proportions of the dog and abstracts from them. Consequently, the work is a pleasing combination of intuitive response, to animal form and geometric simplification, sympathetically expressed in semi-abstract terms.

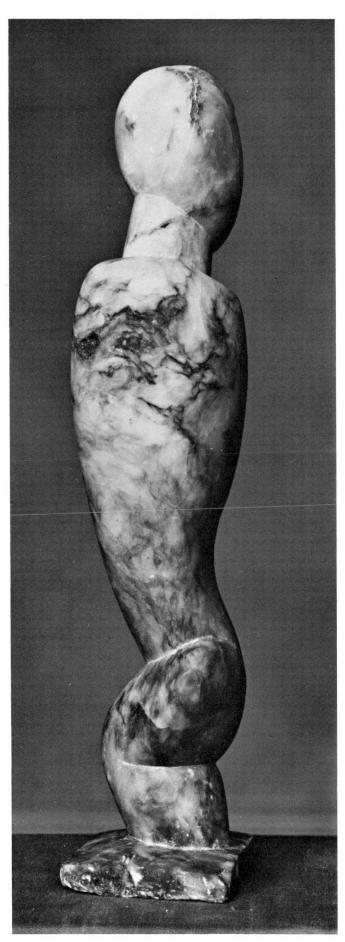

57
IMP

1914. London, Tate Gallery. Veined alabaster. No casts.
16 ×3½ in. Exhibited: London, Goupil Gallery 1915
(No. 96); London, Memorial exhibition 1918 (No. 28);
Leeds 1943 (No. 77); London, Arts Council 1956 (No. 27).

This sculpture shows much of the simplification of form which had concerned Gaudier for several months, but the quality of the stone and the foreshortening of the legs gives the whole figure an uncommitted softness, unlike some of the other carvings of this period. The static pose of the figure gave Gaudier little opportunity for exploration of the stone and the absence of human detail, except on the head, is best described by Pound as, 'an inconclusive statement'.

This sculpture does not appear in Gaudier's *List of Works*.

58. CHARM

1914. Ezra Pound collection. Green stone. Six casts in bronze. 4 ×3½ in. Exhibited: London, Vorticists exhibition 1915 (No. c); London, Memorial exhibition 1918 (No. 22). Photograph taken from the cover of Pound, 1.

This example is one of a number of charms or ornaments described by Gaudier in his *List of Works*. They were obviously popular among his friends and several different designs have come to light over the years. Bronze casts have been made of some stone charms and ornaments, whereas others have been cut directly out of the metal. Gaudier details these on 14 August 1914 as two paperweights, £5 each, with Hulme; one green marble paperweight; one green marble ornament with Ezra Pound; one brass paperweight and design in plaster with Roger Fry. In the *List of Works* Hulme is recorded as also having six half-polished bronze casts of an alabaster carving.

59
MEN WITH BOWL

1914. Plaster (destroyed). Four casts in bronze. 12 ×10 in. Exhibited: Cardiff 1953 (No. 7).

This sculpture directly derives from the artist's studies of primitive sculpture, and illustrates how he developed these influences. This work should be regarded as an exercise, since it refers so closely to its points of origin.
It also serves to illustrate how, by reproducing Gaudier's work in bronze, after his death, some sculptures have achieved a recognition beyond those intended by the artist. Gaudier described this work as 'a study of the primitive so that I may carve stone with more purpose.'

Below:
Tribal sculpture from Africa.

60
GARDEN ORNAMENT 2

1914. London, Tate Gallery. Clay (destroyed). Four bronze casts, one plaster cast. 25 ×8½ in. Exhibited: London, Memorial exhibition 1918 (No. 103); Leeds 1943 (No. 81); Cardiff 1953 (No. 5); Orléans 1956 (No. 72).

This garden ornament and No. 61 were modelled by the artist as maquettes for stone carvings commissioned through the Omega workshops by Lady Hamilton. The sculptures were not completed and the stone for the carvings remained, almost untouched, outside the artist's studio after he left England to fight for France. Both models show direct influences from Gaudier's study of primitive sculpture and are obviously closely developed from ideas explored in sculptures such as *Men with Bowl* (No. 59).

61
GARDEN ORNAMENT 3
*1914. Cambridge University, Kettle's
Yard. Clay/plaster. Nine casts in
bronze — one in lead. 14½×11 in.
Exhibited: Leeds 1943 (No. 82);
Cardiff 1953 (No. 6); London, Arts
Council 1956 (No. 21); London, Folio
Society 1964 (No. 1); London,
Marlborough Gallery 1965 (No. 95).*

See note to No. 60.

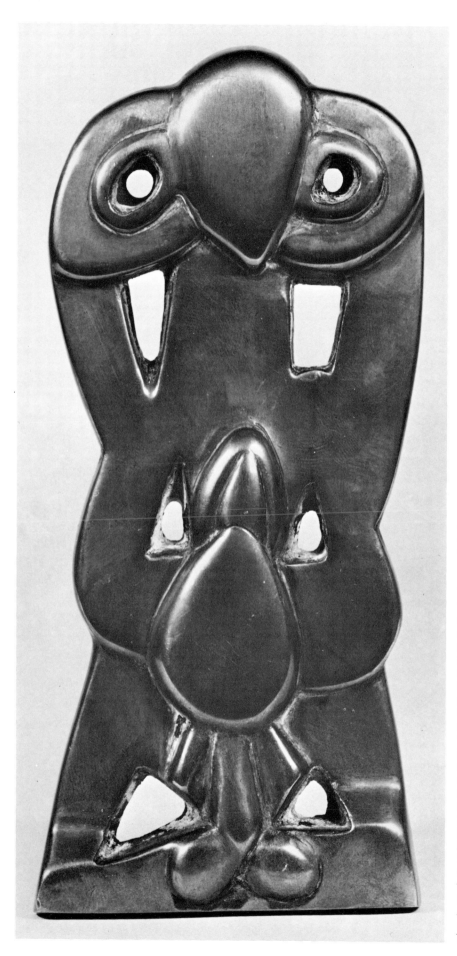

62
DOOR-KNOCKER (Two versions)

1914. Cambridge University, Kettle's Yard. Brass. At least twelve casts from both origin[ ] in bell metal. $6\frac{7}{8} \times 3\frac{1}{4}$ in. Exhibited: London, Allied Artists' exhibition 1914 (Nos 1288 an[ ] 1349); Cardiff 1953 (No. 12); Orléans 1956 (No. 4); London, Arts Council 1956 (No. 2[ ]

There is a great deal of confusion relating to these two door-knockers and the number of casts that exist. Gaudier in his *List of Works* clearly described two different door-knocker[ ] the one 7 in. long, the other 8 in. long, as cu[ ] directly in bronze and polished. Since many casts have been made it is difficult now to determine which are the original door-knock[ ] and which are casts. It seems likely that the Cambridge University door-knockers, from which casts such as the Tate Gallery's were taken, is one of the originals. There is no evidence of any other door-knocker which could be certainly identified as a second original cast. The door-knockers are similar t[ ] charms and ornaments, but their sophisticati[ ] of abstraction of design elevates them above the level of mere ornaments to become more serious sculptures. In his review of the Allied Artists' Association Exhibition Gaudier wrote his own work, 'The door-knocker is an instan[ ] of an abstract design seeming to amplify the value of an object as such. No more cupids riding mermaids, garlands, curtains, stuck anywhere.' The technique is unusual: the obj[ ] is not cast but carved direct out of solid brass The forms gain in sharpness and rigidity.

63A. BRASS TOY

63B. TORPEDO FISH

64. FISH (Not illustrated)
65A & B. KNUCKLE-DUSTER (Two versions)

1914. 63A Private collection; 63B Private collection; 64 Ezra Pound collection; 65B London, Mercury Gallery. Cut brass/bronze; No. 63A — two casts in bronze; No. 63B — nine casts in bronze; Nos 64 and 65 A & B — number of casts not known, although at least one other knuckle-duster of different shape and size does exist. Exhibited: London, Allied Artists' exhibition 1914 (No. 1346, which of 63A or B, or 64 not known); London, Memorial exhibition 1918 (Nos 23, 34, 26).

As with the door-knockers, much confusion surrounds the small ornaments; all express an abstract design and were worked directly into small pieces of metal. Gaudier's *List of Works* provides the best reference in relation to the sculptures and he details them:

Ornament torpille bronze cisele,	6″ ×2 ×1½.	£2.	T. E. Hulme
do. meme modele plâtre	do.		Gaudier Brzeska
Poisson bronze cisele	2″ ×¾	10/–	Mrs Kibblewhite
Medaille fer perfore et cisele	4″ diametre	10/–	T. E. Hulme
Medaille bronze cisele et perfore	4″ diametre	£1. 5. 0.	inconnu

Knuckle-dusters are not included in this list but references in Sophie's diary[1] are made to the knuckle-dusters he cut for Hulme and Lewis.

1. Sophie's diary. Essex University collection.

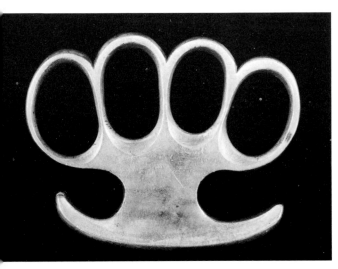

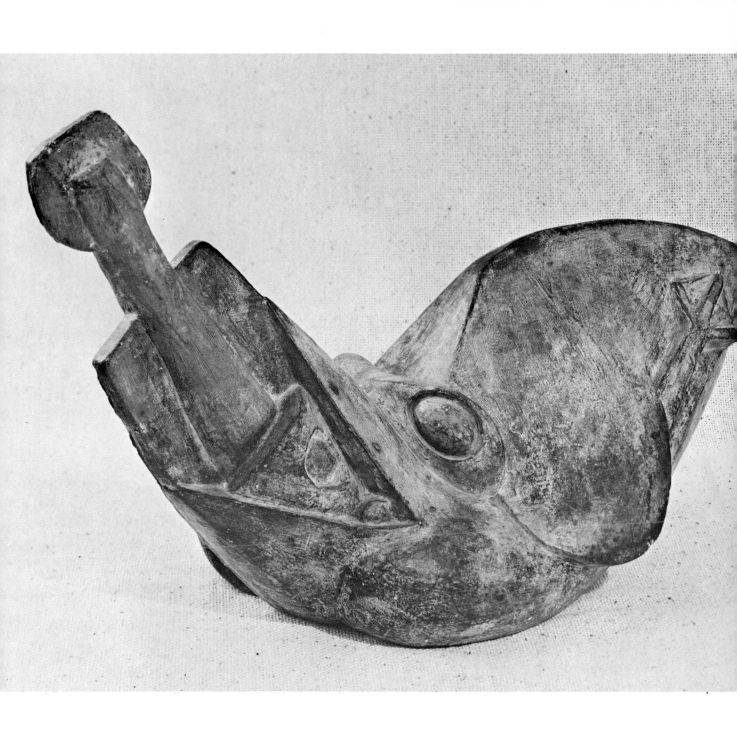

66. BIRD SWALLOWING A FISH

1914. Cambridge University, Kettle's Yard. Plaster. Thirteen casts in bronze (at least).
12½×23¾ in. Exhibited: London, Allied Artists' exhibition 1914 (No. 1345); London,
Memorial exhibition 1918 (No. 95); Cardiff 1953 (No. 1).

Almost certainly this work is the statement which finally established in Gaudier's own
mind a rejection of purely geometric expression in sculpture. This work is a dynamic
fusion of organic and geometric-mechanical form and design. Its achievement was for
Gaudier an important solution to many problems relating to his own developing style,
and it allowed him the freedom to emerge through the pressures of Hulme and Lewis for
a solely geometric sculptural ideal.

Pound states that as a result of his own solution to these problems in his sculptures,
Gaudier planned to write an article on 'The Need of Organic Forms.'

In its concept this sculpture broke new ground and is one of Gaudier's most
significant statements.

67. SEATED WOMAN

*1914. Paris, Musée d'Art Moderne. Marble. Seven casts in bronze. 18½×13½×8½ in.
Exhibited: London, Memorial exhibition 1918 (No. 80); Stadt Bielefeld 1969 (No. 14).*

This sculpture can be seen to have a close affinity with both *Red Stone Dancer* and
Maternity (No. 44). It is noticeable that this work is less abstract and more refined than
these other two sculptures and in the organization of the arms, and their position in
relationship to the head, we have a repetition of Gaudier's involvement with the
interplay of these masses. This sculpture expresses all the artist's ideas about the
simplification of planes as related to masses and as such is one of his most complete and
considered statements. The treatment of the marble is professional and sympathetic and
shows, as did *Red Stone Dancer*, that Gaudier had developed a sensitive response to
stone and was working fully within the material.

68
BIRDS ERECT

1914. New York, Museum of Modern Art.
Limestone. One cast simulated stone. 26⅝×14 in.
Exhibited: London, Memorial exhibition 1918
(No. 56); London, Arts Council 1956 (No. 30).

This carving, the artist's last major work, draws
together most of his earlier ideas and at the same
time anticipates new problems. The sculpture has
an organic structure, previously explored in a
number of his carvings, but achieves a unique
quality in the interrelationship of surface, planes
and masses. The sculpture expresses an inner
awareness of structure, growth and strength. Its
interdependent forms are individually poised and
contoured to give the sculpture a natural beauty.
His last major sculpture, this work achieves a
complete originality.

69
CARVED TOOTHBRUSH HANDLE

1914. Mr R. Bevan collection. Bone.
No casts. 6¾×⅞ in. Exhibited: London,
Memorial exhibition 1918 (No. 28A);
London, Arts Council 1956 (No. 31).

Contrary to popular belief, this
sculpture was carved by the artist
while still in England and sold to
Mrs Bevan, the mother of the present
owner, for ten shillings. It appears in
his *List of Works* of 9 July 1914 as
having been cut from a toothbrush
handle which was then smoked. Like
the 'toys' which he cut for T. E. Hulme
and Ezra Pound, this carving explores
Gaudier's interest in geometric pattern
and design and, as such, is a good
example of the artist's exploration of
these ideas.

01. SELF-PORTRAIT

No photograph known. Mentioned by Gaudier in correspondence of 1910. Given to an Italian woodcarver in Paris. Whereabouts not known.

02. MATERNITY

1913. Location unknown. Plaster. Exhibited: London, Memorial exhibition 1918 (No. 1, La Mendiante. Lent by T. Leman Hare Esq.).

The sculpture appears in Gaudier's *List of Works*: 'Maternité' statuette platre 1½' Lant a per près. £3. T. Leman Hare. 35 Pembroke Road Kensington.'

03. WEEPING WOMAN

1913. Location unknown. Alabaster (bas relief). No casts known. About 12 ×4 in.

All that is known about this sculpture is contained in two written statements, one by Gaudier in his *List of Works*:
  'Tous objets en pierre sont tailles directement sans modèles ni mise au point. Femme pleurante, bas relief, albâtre donné J. Cournos Kensington.'
The other in the autobiography of J. Cournos, quoting Gaudier:
  'The size and shape of the alabaster were responsible for my making her a sentimental woman weeping.'
Gift by Gaudier to Cournos and subsequently sold for $750 to Mrs H. Payne Whitney.

02

04. HEAD OF A MAN

1912. Location unknown. Bath stone (semi-relief). About 15 in. high. Exhibited: London, Memorial exhibition 1918 (No. 43, Head of a Man, stone 1912).

Said by Pound, 1, following page 52, plate XIV, to be Head of Christ since destroyed by the sculptor. It is referred to by Ede, 1930, plate XXX, and exhibited Leeds 1943, No. 71, as head of a man.

05. MASK OF MARIA CARMI

No photographs known. Mentioned by Gaudier in correspondence of 1912 as a gift to Lovat Fraser.

04

06. PORTRAIT OF A BOY

1912. Seravezza marble. Exhibited: London, Memorial exhibition 1918 (No. 9, 'Bas relief' marble, 1912–13, lent by Mrs Kinnear).

The sculpture appears in Gaudier's *List of Works*: ' "Garcon" bas-relief Marbre Seravezza circa 1½' haut ⅞'' large £5. 5. 0. M. Kinnear old cow Regents Park.'

07. CHEETAH

1912. Private collection. Painted plaster. Exhibited: London, Memorial exhibition 1918 (No. 19, lent by Lovat Fraser).

The sculpture appears in Gaudier's *List of Wprks*: 'Animal (cheetah) pâtre peint. 18'' long 6'' haut 2'' epais. £2.' Also referred to in a letter dated 28.10.1912.

08. INFANT HERCULES

1913.

Referred to in Gaudier's notebooks.

09. FOOTBALL PLAYER

1913. London, custody of Victoria and Albert Museum, 2 June 1916. Letter. Location now unknown.

010. VENUS

1913.

Referred to in Gaudier's notebooks.

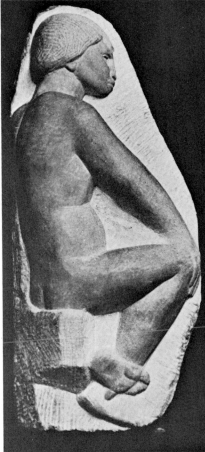

06

07

011. POTTERY HEAD

Cambridge University, Kettle's Yard. Glazed white. Possibly Omega workshops. No casts. About 4 in. high.

012. ALABASTER CARVING

Unfinished. Cambridge University, Kettle's Yard, No. 36. No casts. About 6 in. high.

013. EROTIC GROUP

1913/14.
Referred to in Gaudier's notebooks.

014. SMALL TOYS

1913. Green marble.
Mentioned in Gaudier's *List of Works*.

015. BIRD

1914.
Referred to in Gaudier's notebooks.

016. MATERNITY

1915. Carved for Captain Menager from a German rifle-butt. Wood.
Mentioned by Gaudier in correspondence from the trenches.

017. GROUP (Two sculptures)

1915. Wood and stone. Made in trenches, Ede, 1, p. 206.

018. CHICAN

1910. Plaster. $1\frac{1}{2}$ times life size, with exaggerated characteristics.
Referred to in Gaudier's notebooks.

019. PORTRAIT OF MOTHER ROUZEAU

1914. Plaster. $1\frac{1}{2}$ times life size, with exaggerated characteristics.
Mentioned in Gaudier's *List of Works*.

020. VENUS

1913.
Mentioned in Gaudier's *List of Works*.

021. INSECT STATUETTE

1914. Portland and Bath stone. $2\frac{1}{2}$ in. high. Exhibited: London, Allied Artists' 1914.
Mentioned in Gaudier's *List of Works*.

011

12

022. HEAD OF A CHILD

1913. Portland stone. Masque. Twice life size.

Mentioned in Gaudier's *List of Works*.

023. ONE TOTEM IN BLACK SLATE

1914. Private collection.

Gift to E. Pound.

024. FIGURE STUDY

1912/13. Purchased by Leicester Galleries from Dr G. A. Jellicoe; sold to Dr N. Goodman 1933; gift to Victoria and Albert Museum from Dr Goodman. Bronze. $4\frac{1}{2} \times 2 \times 1\frac{7}{8}$ in.

This sculpture does not appear in any list of works by the artist.

025. MONKEY

1912. Plaster. Two bronze casts. About $8\frac{1}{2}$ in. high. Exhibited: London, Memorial exhibition 1918 (No. 20). Plaster reproduced in Brodzky, p. 67. Lent to Leeds, Temple Newsam exhibition No. 60.

026. FALLEN WORKMAN

1912. Gift by H. S. Ede to Musée des Beaux Arts, Orléans. Plaster. Lost.

Similar to No. 17.

027. SERPENTS ENTWINED

1912. Owned by H. S. Ede 1943. Sent to Leeds exhibition by H. S. Ede, 17 June 1943; since untraced. Wax.

028. MASK OF A MAN'S HEAD

1912. Owned by H. S. Ede, 1943. Wax.

029. AMOUR

1913. Sometime collection of Mrs A. Kohnstamm. Alabaster on gilt background. 18 × 5 in. Exhibited: Manchester exhibition (No. 34). Lent by A. Kohnstamm. Reproduced Brodzky, opp. p. 97.

The sculpture appears in Gaudier's *List of Works*: 'Amour bas relief garcon albâtre baille directe circa i' haut 3'' ou 4'' large £6. Al. Kohnstamm, Hampstead. demi poli fond doré.'

025

026

31

030. PORTRAIT BUST OF FRANK HARRIS

1913. Plaster.
Gaudier refers to this sculpture in a letter to Dr Uhlemayr dated 12 March 1913.

031. POT À FLEURS
032. DEUX DEMI-STATUETTES
033. PLÂTEAU

The three pieces of sculpture commissioned by R. Macfarlane Cocks. See Chapter 2, footnote 13.

034. HEAD OF A WRESTLER

Cambridge University, Kettle's Yard.

035. SEATED FIGURE

Reproduced in the *Burlington Magazine* 1916. Drawing also reproduced.

035

035

ORIGINAL
WRITINGS by
HENRI GAUDIER

THE VORTEX

SCULPTURAL energy is the mountain.

Sculptural feeling is the appreciation of masses in relation.

Sculptural ability is the defining of these masses by planes.

The PALEOLITHIC VORTEX resulted in the decoration of the Dordogne caverns.

Early stone-age man disputed the earth with animals. His livelihood depended on the hazards of the hunt — his greatest victory the domestication of a few species.

Out of the minds primordially preoccupied with animals Fonts-de-Gaume gained its procession of horses carved in the rock. The driving power was life in the absolute — the plastic expression the fruitful sphere.

The sphere is thrown through space; it is the soul and object of the vortex —

The intensity of existence had revealed to man a truth of form — his manhood was strained to the highest potential — his energy brutal — HIS OPULENT MATURITY WAS CONVEX.

The acute flight subsided at the birth of the three primary civilizations. It always retained more intensity East.

The HAMITE VORTEX of Egypt, the land of plenty —

Man succeeded in his far reaching speculations — Honour to the divinity!

Religion pushed him to the use of the VERTICAL which inspires awe. His gods were self-made, he built them in his image, and RETAINED AS MUCH OF THE SPHERE AS COULD ROUND THE SHARPNESS OF THE PARALLELOGRAM.

He preferred the pyramid to the mastaba.

The fair Greek felt this influence across the middle sea.

The fair Greek saw himself only. HE petrified his own semblance.

HIS SCULPTURE WAS DERIVATIVE, his feeling for form secondary. The absence of direct energy lasted for a thousand years.

The Indians felt the hamitic influence through Greek spectacles. Their extreme temperament inclined towards asceticism, admiration of non-desire as a balance against abuse produced a kind of sculpture without new form perception — and which is the result of the peculiar.

VORTEX OF BLACKNESS AND SILENCE.

PLASTIC SOUL IS INTENSITY OF LIFE BURSTING THE PLANE.

The Germanic barbarians were verily whirled by the mysterious need of acquiring new arable lands. They moved restlessly, like strong oxen stampeding.

The SEMITIC VORTEX was the lust of war. The men of Elam, of Assur, of Bebel and the Kheta, the men of Armenia and those of Canaan had to slay each other cruelly for the possession of fertile valleys. Their gods sent them the vertical direction, the earth, the SPHERE.

They elevated the sphere in splendid squatness and created the HORIZONTAL.

From Sargon to Amir-nasir-pal men built man-headed bulls in horizontal flight-walk. Men flayed their captives alive and erected howling lions: THE ELONGATED HORIZONTAL SPHERE BUTTRESSED ON FOUR COLUMNS, and their kingdoms disappeared.

Christ flourished and perished in Yudah.

Christianity gained Africa, and from the seaports of the Mediterranean it won the Roman Empire.

The stampeding Franks came into violent contact with it as well as the Greco-Roman tradition.

They were swamped by the remote reflections of the two vortices of the West.

Gothic sculpture was but a faint echo of the HAMITO-SEMITIC energies through Roman traditions, and it lasted half a thousand years, and it wilfully divagated again into the Greek derivation from the land of Amen-Ra.

VORTEX OF A VORTEX!!

VORTEX IS THE POINT ONE AND INDIVISIBLE!

VORTEX IS ENERGY! and it gave forth SOLID EXCREMENTS in the quattro e cinque cento, LIQUID until the seventeenth century, GASES whistle till now. THIS is the history of form value in the West until the FALL OF IMPRESSIONISM.

The black-haired men who wandered through the pass of Khotan into the valley of the YELLOW RIVER lived peacefully tilling their lands, and they grew prosperous.

Their paleolithic feeling was intensified. As gods they had themselves in the persons of their human ancestors — and of the spirits of the horse and of the land and the grain.

THE SPHERE SWAYED.

THE VORTEX WAS ABSOLUTE.

The Shang and Chow dynasties produced the convex bronze vases.

The features of Tac-t'ie were inscribed inside the square with the rounded corners — the centuple spherical frog presided over the inverted truncated cone that is the bronze war drum.

THE VORTEX WAS INTENSE MATURITY. Maturity is fecundity — they grew numerous and it lasted for six thousand years.

The force relapsed and they accumulated wealth, forsook their work, and after losing their form-understanding through the Hand and T'ang dynasties, they founded the Ming and found artistic ruin and sterility.

THE SPHERE LOST SIGNIFICANCE AND THEY ADMIRED THEMSELVES.

During their great period off-shoots from their race had landed on another continent. After many wanderings some tribes settled on the highlands of Yukatan and Mexico.

When the Ming were losing their conception, these neo-Mongols had a flourishing state. Through the strain of warfare they submitted the Chinese sphere to horizontal treatment such as the Semites had done. Their cruel nature and temperament supplied them with a stimulant: THE VORTEX OF DESTRUCTION.

Besides these highly developed peoples there lived on the world other races inhabiting Africa and the Ocean islands.

When we first knew them they were very near the paleolithic stage. Though they were not so much dependent upon animals their expenditure of energy was wide, for they began to till the land and practice crafts rationally, and they fell into contemplation before their sex: the site of their great energy: THEIR CONVEX MATURITY.

They pulled the sphere lengthways and made the cylinder, this is the VORTEX OF FECUNDITY, and it has left us the masterpieces that are known as love charms.

The soil was hard, material difficult to win from nature, storms frequent, as also fevers and other epidemics. They got frightened: This is the VORTEX OF FEAR, its mass is the POINTED CONE, its masterpiece the fetishes.

and WE moderns: Epstein, Brancusi, Archipenko, Dunikowski, Modigliani, and myself, through the incessant struggle in the complex city, have likewise to spend much energy.

The knowledge of our civilisation embraces the world, we have mastered the elements.

We have been influenced by what we like most, each according to his own individuality, we have crystalized the sphere into the cube, we have made a combination of all the possible shaped masses — concentrating them to express our abstract thoughts of conscious superiority.

Will and consciousness are our
VORTEX.

ALLIED ARTISTS' ASSOCIATION LTD.
Holland Park Hall.
By HENRI GAUDIER BRZESKA.

I AM in a perilous position. I am on the year's staff of the association, an exhibitor and the personal friend of many artists who show their works. In some quarters I am supposed to write an official whitewashing account; many readers will accuse me of self-adulation and praising of a sect — for all these people I have the greatest contempt.

SCULPTURE

I specially begin with this virile art. The critics as a whole ignore it — place it always last — excusing themselves by the kind sentence: 'It is not lack of good-will but lack of space which prevents me from,' etc. etc. They also prate endlessly about sculpture being separated from her mother art: Architecture — poor child! If they had not lost their manhood they would find that sculpture and architecture are one and the same art. On many occasions sculptors have erected buildings to place their statues. On many occasions artists like Epstein, Brancusi and myself would easily build palaces in harmony with their statuary. The architecture that would result would be quite original, new, primordial. A professional critic's mind cannot see beyond vile revivals of Greco-Roman and Gothic styles. A professional critic when organizing a provincial exhibition catalogues the 'group in red alabaster' of one man as the 'group in white marble' of another — it proves their omniscience.

The sculpture I admire is the work of master craftsmen. Every inch of the surface is won at the point of the chisel — every stroke of the hammer is a physical and a mental effort. No more arbitrary translations of a design in any material. They are fully aware of the different qualities and possibilities of woods, stones, and metals. Epstein, whom I consider the foremost in the small number of good sculptors in Europe, lays particular stress on this. Brancusi's greatest pride is his consciousness of being an accomplished workman. Unfortunately Epstein, who has been a constant exhibitor at the A.A.A., is absent this year. A work in marble by Brancusi is catalogued, but up to the present it has not arrived. It is a great pity, for I intended to dwell at length on the merits of this statue. The number of people who are at all furthering their sculptural expression is thus reduced to Zadkin and myself.

ZADKIN

is contributing two works in wood — another in stone. I prefer the wooden head. We have here a composition of masses moving in three concentric directions. To be especially admired is the contrast of the deeply undercut hair mass to the undulated surface of the shoulders. This head would be a masterpiece were it not a little spoilt by a very sweet expression. The technique is beautiful — a quality of surface which is seldom seen in wood. The other wood composition is far less satisfactory — it is also sentimental, which spoils the general effect. We get in the stone group *Holy Family* the same heads again — in two instances but in very low relief — half the group is thus tinged with insipidity. A corner of it is well cut and very serene. On the whole Zadkin is pulled between a very flowing, individual conception of form — which some artists call 'lack of form' — and which has the power of emanating great life — and a very strong liking for pretty melancholy — which bores me.

GAUDIER BRZESKA

I have on show a *Boy with a Rabbit* which has been referred to in these columns as an echo of the bronze animals of the Chow dynasty. It is better than they. They had, it is true, a maturity brought by continuous rotundities — my statuette has more monumental concentration — a result of the use of flat and round surfaces. To be appreciated is the relation between the mass of the rabbit and the right arm with that of the rest. The next is a bird. Unfortunately I now see that had the planes of the wings been convex and the forepart thicker the design would have gained in buoyancy and stateliness. The design in alabaster creates an emotion of distinguished melancholy. The design in green marble one of intense reptile life. The door-knocker is an instance of an abstract design serving to amplify the value of an object as such. No more cupids riding mermaids, garlands, curtains — stuck anywhere! The technique is unusual; the object is not cast but carved direct out of solid brass. The forms gain in sharpness and rigidity.

The rest of the sculpture is an agglomeration of Rodin–Maillol mixture and valueless academism — with here and there someone trying to be naughty: curled nubilities and discreet slits.

PAINTING

Lewis's most important work had not arrived when I wrote this. I propose to write another article dealing with it and Brancusi's statue if it comes. Wyndham Lewis has made enormous progress in his painting. The two small abstractions *Night Attack* and *Signalling* are such very complete individual expressions that no praise is sufficient adequately to point out their qualities. These are designs of wilful shapes contained in a whole in motion — and this acquired with the simplest means — ochres and blacks. Lewis's abstractions are of a decided type and their composition is so successful that I feel right in seeing in them the start of a new evolution in painting.

WADSWORTH

is well represented by a 'short flight': a composition of cool tones marvellously embodied in revolving surfaces and masses. His bigger picture, No. 113, gives more pleasure on account of the warmer pigments used and the construction: growing in a corner and balanced at the other by a short mass.

PHELAN GIBB

is hung next to Wadsworth, which makes its poor amorphism and lack of design appear the more. A really poor kind of abstraction half-way between Kandinsky and Picasso of the early stages.

KANDINSKY

presents an 'improvisation,' 'picture with yellow colouring,' and a third, No. 1559. I have been told that he is a very great painter, that his lack of construction is a magnificent quality, that he has hit something very new. Alas, I also know all his twaddle 'of the spiritual in art.' I agree that these colours — set free, so to speak — have an effect of mirth. This is a very slight emotion nevertheless. My temperament does not allow of formless, vague assertions, 'all what is not like me is evil'; so is Kandinsky.

A. DE SOUZA CARDOSO

comes nearer to my feelings. He has as much colour as Kandinsky and of a richer kind in his *Musicien de Nuit*. Whereas Kandinsky always uses the same palette — at least in his works here — Cardoso tones it down to a perfection in his *Jardinier*, a jewel of warm blues agitated in a fresh motion.

KARL HAGEDORN

offers the worst instance of feelingless abstraction — no emotions; no art.

NEVINSON

a futurist painted. It is impressionism using false weapons. The emotions are of a superficial character, merging on the vulgar in the 'syncopation' — union-jacks, lace stockings and other tommy rot. The coloured relief is at least free from this banality — yet there are ciphers and letters — and though the whole is in good movement I do not appreciate it.

People like Miss Dismorr, Miss Saunders and Miss Jones are well worth encouraging in their endeavours towards the new light. With them stops the revolutionary spirit of the exhibition. Before dealing with the rest of the painting I make a digression among applied art. The Rebel art centre has a stand. The Omega shops have the lounge. The Rebel stand is in unity. A desire to employ the most vigorous forms of decoration fills it with fans, scarves, boxes and a table, which are the finest of these objects I have seen.

The spirit in the lounge is one of subtlety. I admire the black and white carpet — the inlaid tables and trays, the pottery. The chairs, the cushions and especially a screen with two natural swans and the hangings of patched work irritate me — there is too much prettiness.

Happily the Rebel stand shows that the new painting is capable of great strength and manliness in decoration.

Though I am not wholly in sympathy with the other painters, I feel it my duty to point out that the rest of the hall is shared by two sections — one composed of able, convinced men admiring natural forms only — and the other of poor academic imitators whose efforts cannot be classified as art even.

There is a transitional body — men starting from nature and getting on the verge of the abstract.

WOLMARK

His two negroes handling carpets make a fine composition. The not so violent colours as usual, the good workmanship, and intensified drawing make of it his best work so far. His smaller *Negro* of duller tones yet, is also very successful. Wolmark argues that his representation helps to receive the emotion purported by the design. This is a difficult question — it must be candidly said that this form of art can co-exist with absolute abstraction and fill one with pleasure.

MISS ROWLEY LEGGETT

in her reclining woman shares apparently the same view. Her colours are fresh and transparent, and as the expression, the human interest at large is very secondary to the composition. I like it very much.

HORACE BRODZKY

sends an able *Still life* and a *Portrait* — the colours are very warm but here I feel the representation to have become the primary quality. A fault of which I accuse the painter is of preferring harsh contrast. A quality I find is his great frankness.

MISS HAMNETT

cares much about representation. It is very interesting to see a portrait of Zadkin, the wood-carver. In this work there are great technical qualities of pastel and drawing — more amplified in the other portrait — where carefully chosen blacks and violets create a very distinguished effect. I see from the qualities of the 'women composition' that the affinities of this artist are coming nearer to a preference for abstract design.

MME R. FINCH

has a good portrait. The greens and reds are finely tempered by the qualities of the face. I recognize here a greater talent than I have ever met in a woman artist. The *Reginald* unhappily does not rank so high as this masterly little head.

Then come the artists more or less closely bound with the Camden Town Group.

MME. KARLOWSKA

has a good picture — a happy composition of figures in a half-circle — figures of secondary importance to the composition — and a great relief with it, the absence of pink atmosphere.

BEVAN

has 'horses' — also an original composition — crossing the surface of the picture at an angle with two contrary movements balanced by a globular crowd. I believe greater enjoyment would be derived from its colours and arrangement had Bevan done away with the notion that he saw horses and men.

VORTEX GAUDIER BRZESKA
(written from the trenches)

I have been fighting for two months and I can now gauge the intensity of life.

Human masses teem and move, are destroyed and crop up again.

Horses are worn out in three weeks, die by the roadside.

Dogs wander, are destroyed, and others come along.

With all the destruction that works around us NOTHING IS CHANGED, EVEN SUPERFICIALLY. **LIFE IS THE SAME STRENGTH**, THE MOVING AGENT THAT PERMITS THE SMALL INDIVIDUAL TO ASSERT HIMSELF.

THE BURSTING SHELLS, the volleys, wire entanglements, projectors, motors, the chaos of battle DO NOT ALTER IN THE LEAST the outline of the hill we are beseiging. A company of PARTRIDGES scuttle along before our very trench.

IT WOULD BE FOLLY TO SEEK ARTISTIC EMOTIONS AMID THESE LITTLE WORKS OF OURS.

THIS PALTRY MECHANISM, WHICH SERVES AS A PURGE TO OVER-NUMEROUS HUMANITY.

THIS WAR IS A GREAT REMEDY.

IN THE INDIVIDUAL IT KILLS ARROGANCE, SELF-ESTEEM, PRIDE.

IT TAKES AWAY FROM THE MASSES NUMBERS UPON NUMBERS OF UNIMPORTANT UNITS, WHOSE ECONOMIC ACTIVITIES BECOME NOXIOUS AS THE RECENT CRISES HAVE SHOWN US.

MY VIEWS ON SCULPTURE REMAIN ABSOLUTELY **THE SAME.**

IT IS THE **VORTEX** OF WILL, OF DECISION, THAT BEGINS.

I SHALL DERIVE MY EMOTIONS SOLELY FROM THE ARRANGEMENT OF SURFACES, I shall present my emotions by the ARRANGEMENT OF MY SURFACES, THE PLANES AND LINES BY WHICH THEY ARE DEFINED.

Just as this hill where the Germans are solidly entrenched, gives me a nasty feeling, solely because its gentle slopes are broken up by earthy-works, which throw long shadows at sunset. Just so shall I get feeling of whatsoever definition, from a statue. ACCORDING TO ITS SLOPES, varied to infinity.

I have made an experiment. Two days ago I pinched from an enemy a Mauser rifle. Its heavy unwieldy shape swamped me with a powerful IMAGE of brutality.

I was in doubt for a long time whether it pleased or displeased me.

I found that I did not like it.

I broke the butt off and with my knife I carved in it a design, through which I tried to express a gentler order of feeling, which I preferred.

BUT I WILL EMPHASIZE that MY DESIGN **got its effect** (just as the gun had) FROM A VERY SIMPLE COMPOSITION OF LINES AND PLANES.

GAUDIER BRZESKA.

List of
Exhibitions

June/July 1913
Allied Artists' Association. Albert Hall, London

October 1913
Royal West of England Academy, Bath

November 1913
International Society of Sculptors, Painters and Gravers. Grosvenor Gallery, London

January 1914
Grafton Group. Alpine Gallery, London

February 1914
London Group. Goupil Gallery, London

20 May 1914
Twentieth Century Art. Whitechapel Gallery, London

July 1914
Allied Artists' Association. Albert Hall, London

March 1915
London Group. Goupil Gallery, London

May 1915
Vorticist exhibition. Doré Gallery, London, and, 1916, Penguin Club, New York

May–June 1918
Memorial exhibition. Leicester Galleries, London

26 June–29 August 1931
Exhibition of Sculptures and Drawings. Temple Newsam, Leeds

27 April–23 May 1931
Exhibition of Drawings and Statues. J. & E. Bumpus. Old Court House, St Marylebone, London

26 June–29 August 1943
Exhibition of Sculpture and Drawings. Temple Newsam, Leeds

24 July–8 August 1953
Sculpture, Painting and Drawings. 62 St Mary Street, Cardiff

17 March–22 April 1956
Henri Gaudier, Sculpteur Orléannais. Musée des Beaux Arts, Orléans

7 December 1955–19 January 1956
Henri Gaudier Brzeska. Arts Council Gallery, 4 St James's Square, London

5 March–13 April 1961
Henri Gaudier Brzeska — Drawings. Meridian Avenue, Miami Beach, Florida

1–30 October 1962
Gaudier Brzeska. Leicester Galleries, London

27 April–22 May 1964
Gaudier Brzeska: Sculpture and Drawings. Folio Society, 6 Stratford Place, London

4–30 October 1965
Gaudier Brzeska and Jacob Epstein. Tib Lane Gallery, Manchester

1965
Gaudier Brzeska. Marlborough Gallery, London

22 November–17 December 1966
Gaudier Brzeska drawings. Waddington Galleries, London

12 March–6 April 1968
Gaudier Brzeska drawings. Mercury Gallery, London

1969
Henri Gaudier Brzeska. Stadt Bielefeld, Germany.

1972
Henri Gaudier Brzeska. Edinburgh, Scottish National Gallery of Modern Art

Exhibitions since 1972:
Mercury Gallery, London, 1975
Mercury Gallery, London, 1977
Middlesbrough Museum and Art Gallery, 1977
Towner Art Gallery, Eastbourne, 1977
The Scottish Gallery, Edinburgh, 1977
Mappin Art Gallery, Sheffield, 1977
Bradford Art Gallery, 1977
Gruenebaum Gallery, New York, U.S.A., 1977
Waddington Galleries, Montreal, Toronto, Canada, 1978

Bibliography

The entries in this bibliography are listed in chronological order of publictation.

Pound, E.: *Gaudier Brzeska*. John Lane, 1916

H. Gaudier Brzeska. (Portfolio of reproductions of 20 drawings.) Ovid Press, 1919/20

Ede, H. S.: *A Life of Gaudier Brzeska*. Heinemann, 1930

Ede, H. S.: *Savage Messiah*. Heinemann, 1931

Ede, H. S.: *Savage Messiah*. The Literary Guild, New York, 1931

Brodzky, H.: *Henri Gaudier Brzeska*. Faber and Faber, 1933

Brodzky, H.: *Gaudier Brzeska Drawings*. Faber and Faber, 1946

Ede, H. S.: *Un grand artiste méconnu: Henri Gaudier Brzeska 'Le Jardin des Arts'*, Paris, 1955

Varin, R., and Auzas-Provost, J.: *Henri Gaudier, Sculpteur Orléannais*. Musée des Beaux Arts, Orleans, 1956

Gaudier Brzeska. With a Vortex Manifesto by E. Pound. All Insegna Del Pesce D'oro Milan, 1957

Pound, E.: *Gaudier Brzeska*. Reprint. Marvell Press, Yorkshire, 1960

Levy, M.: *Gaudier Brzeska*. Cory, Adams, Mackay, 1965

PERIODICALS

Apollo, January 1963: 'Lewis and Vorticists'. October 1964: 'The Ideal Home Rumpus'. March 1970: 'The Omega Workshops and Vorticism'

Apple (Second & Third Quarter), 1919, pp. 123–156: 'Drawings', by Gaudier

Apple (First Quarter), 1920: 'The Curse', by E. Pound

Apple (Fourth Quarter), 1920: 'The Bacchante'

Apple (Fifth Quarter), 1921: 'Portrait'

Art Chronicle, Vol. IX, No. 107, 6 December 1912: p. 57

Arts Magazine, January 1960, pp. 26–9: 'Brancusi'

Blast 1 and 2, June 1914; July 1915

Burlington Magazine, Ed. XXIX, 1916: p. 209 and 'H. Gaudier Brzeska' by Roger Fry

Cambridge Review, No. 2197, May 1970

Egoist, 1914: 16 February; 16 March; 15 June; 15 July; 15 August; 1 September.

English Review, October 1919: Article by Hueffer on Gaudier

Esquire Chicago 11, 3 August 1934: pp. 73–4

Evening Standard, 19 October 1931: Harold Nicholson on Nina Hamnett

Fortnightly Review, XCVI, 1 September 1914: pp. 461–71

Horizon, August 1942: pp. 128–40

Le Jardin Des Arts, No. 13, November 1955: 'Une Grande Artiste Méconnu'

Listener, 7 July 1963: pp. 305–07, 'Henry Moore Talking'

New Age, 4 February 1918; 23 May, 1918; 14 January 1921

Poetry 111, 6 March 1914: pp. 220–23, 'Homage to Wilfred Blunt'

Reedy's Mirror, XXV, 32, 18 August 1916: pp. 535–36

Rhythm, 1 September 1912

Studio, Vol. 162, August 1961: pp. 48–51

Studio International, Vol. 173, April 1967: 'Futurism and Vorticism'

Sketch, 25 March 1914: Reproduction of *Stags*

Time, July 1965

Index

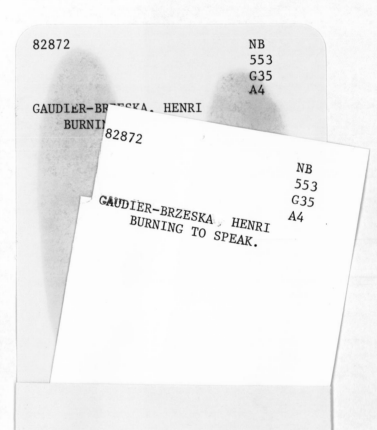